THE PRETENDERS

PRETENDERS

WITH HYNDESIGHT

BY MIKE WRENN

Omnibus Press
London/New York/Sydney/Cologne

Edited by Chris Charlesworth
Art Editor Tony Foo
Picture Research by Debbie Dorman
Project and typesetting co-ordinated by Caroline Watson

ISBN 0.7119.1772.8
Order No: OP45269

Exclusive distributors:

Book Sales Limited,
8/9 Frith Street,
London W1V 5TZ, UK.

Music Sales Corporation,
225 Park Avenue South,
New York, NY 10003, USA.

Music Sales Pty Limited,
120 Rothschild Avenue,
Rosebery, NSW 2018, Australia.

To the Music Trade only:
Music Sales Limited,
8/9 Frith Street,
London W1V 5TZ, UK.

Picture credits: Adrian Boot p11(L&R), 23, 27, 35(R), 51, 62, 91,
London Features Int. p2, 4, 7, 9, 10, 12, 14, 18(L&R), 19, 22, 25, 28, 30, 31, 32, 39,
41, 44, 46, 47, 49, 50, 52, 56, 58, 59, 64, 65, 69, 70, 71, 73, 80, 87(L&R), 88, 93, 95.
Barry Plummer p20, 43.
Pictorial Press Ltd. p76, 79, 98.
Ebet Roberts p84, 85.
Paul Slattery p6, 24, 36, 37, 38.

Every effort has been made to trace the copyright holders
of the photographs in this book but one or two were
unreachable. We would be grateful if the photographers
concerned would contact us.

Typeset by Capital Setters, London.

Printed in England by Courier International Ltd, Tiptree, Essex.

CONTENTS

> I read something in the paper the other day that explains it all quite well. There was a bloke driving down a road in South Africa, and a girl in the next car had a pet snake. He asked her if she minded if he touched the snake. She said 'no', so he leant over and bit a chunk off its tail. In court a week later he was heard to say, 'I'm a jazz drummer . . . I've got to be free.' That's the way it is in rock 'n' roll. You've got to have a certain amount of irresponsibility, and it *is* to do with drugs, because drugs can *never* be safe.

Martin Chambers, **1984**

CHAPTER ONE

Standing On The Corner

MS HYNDE GETTING PRECIOUS OVER HER SKIN CONDITION.

PHILADELPHIA, AUTUMN 1981: Chrissie sinks back in her chair, dragging on a cigarette. Looking pale and drawn, her smudged eyeliner and sunken cheeks belie the fact she's the newest sex symbol of the post-punk era.

Her band's second album, the imaginatively titled 'Pretenders II', has just been unleashed to rave reviews in the States. Predictably, no one in Britain likes it, no one except the record-buying public that is. Happily they're playing America right now . . . or rather they were.

Eight weeks into a sell-out US tour, Chrissie has just learned of an accident concerning drummer Martin Chambers. Ensconced in his hotel suite prior to the evening's performance, the rhythm machine had apparently thrown a wobbly with his wife and, as a result, managed to slash his hand against a defenceless light bulb. The injury requires 35 stitches, the light bulb needs replacing and the tour has to be scrapped. No one is very happy.

After two months on the road, The Pretenders have just about covered the cost of this, the latest in a long haul of promotional treks. The extra scheduled month would have put them into profit.

Guitarist Jimmy Honeyman-Scott threatens to take Chambers to court – he's probably joking. Bass player Pete Farndon threatens death to all light bulbs – *he* probably isn't. Chrissie Hynde just shrugs her shoulders. **"So we lose out on a few dollars, so what? It's only money,"** she tells one roaming reporter. **"Plenty worse things happen in life, you know. Plenty worse things happen in rock 'n' roll for that matter!"**

Indeed.

Born in 1952 and raised in Akron, Ohio, Christine Elaine Hynde was obsessed with music throughout her childhood. Her parents would have preferred it otherwise of course but, then again, wouldn't they all.

Not rich, not poor, Chrissie's roots lie in blue collar suburbia, though she prefers the term 'collarless' – it's a pop star's prerogative. **"My dad had been in the Marines,"** she details. **"My mother's father was a cop. But there wasn't like a military vibe or anything. It was just very America, y'know. Nice. My parents are the people that vote for Nixon and Reagan."**

Initially influenced by a jazz-loving brother named Terry, the would-be rock 'n' roller started out by experimenting with the the saxophone. If her brother had been a drummer, then she'd probably have done that. But a sax was available, so sax it was.

Chrissie enjoyed the challenge the instrument provided, but it clearly wasn't her scene. Indeed it wasn't until she was 14-years-old that she first realised what kind of music *did* turn her on.

A keen fan of regional radio, Chrissie still remembers making plans to attend the Annual Appreciation Day of a local station called WHOL. For the uninitiated, such events are somewhat akin to the infamous Radio One Roadshow – only considerably less crass. Chrissie was impressed.

"I'd never been to anything like it," she enthuses. **"They held it in this big amusement park, and had all these people like Mitch Ryder and The Detroit Wheels playing. Jimmy McCartney, who was on guitar, just blew my mind totally. I just thought, fuck me, ha-ha! They even faked this fist fight on stage, only I didn't know it was phoney, so I stayed on for the next show and *whoops* . . . same fight. I tell you, from then on my fate was sealed."**

The impact on this impressionable teenager was staggering, and she immediately started practising a new instrument – the ukulele! Within a couple of years six strings had replaced the limiting four, and Chrissie began to jam with local musicians.

BRASS IN POCKET: CHRISSIE CASHES IN.

Her favourite performers at this time were principally those she'd discovered through black radio. BB King, Jackie Wilson, Bobby Womack and James Brown provided a central core of listening pleasure – although many others would soon be reflected in the style of her first real band. This was called Sat. Sun. Mat. and, although the moniker was diabolical, there's at least *one* other reason for their momentous anonymity. They were crap. Interestingly though, the line-up did include another young star in the making, keyboard player Mark Mothersbaugh. Destined for even lesser things, Mark would later turn up in the ranks of Devo. They may have been crap too, but the pay was considerably better.

While most of her girl friends flirted with boys, Chrissie focused all her attention on rock 'n' roll, and tried to get to see every band that ever played her territory.

"One of the first I saw would have been The Rolling Stones," the star now recalls. **"I caught them in Cleveland, Ohio, round about 1966. Brian Jones was wearing plaid boots. Keith Richards and Bill Wyman were wearing two suits but they'd swopped jackets, so Keith**

was in yellow trousers, which I'd never seen before. I remember Jagger did a fantastic bow when they finished 'Lady Jane', which Brian sat down and played dulcimer on. And at one point in the show a girl threw a note up on the stage at Bill Wyman, who had a very cool stage persona. With his left hand he reached up and plucked this note out of the air and put it in his pocket, and kept on playing, which I thought was *well* cool. I can't remember the mystic music very well, probably because the PA system was drowned out by girls screaming. The McCoys were the support group. They were from Ohio and they had that song 'Hang On Sloopy'. It was a memorable day for me!"

If The Rolling Stones opened her heart to British music, it was The Kinks who would later steal it, as Ray Davies' well respected group quickly became Chrissie's favourite band of the period.

"I can remember driving a hundred miles to see The Kinks when I was 18 or so," says Chrissie. **"After the show my girl friend and I hung around to watch them leave the building – we must have been out there for over an hour. And then they came out and, as he walked by me – I was sitting on the kerb – Ray Davies dropped his towel where I was sitting. And he bent over and picked it up and he looked at me, and I looked at him, and he said hello. So I was delighted."**

"AND WITH MY NEXT ADVANCE, I'M BUYING SOME GLOVES!" CHRISSIE GIVES US THAT CHILLING LOOK.

HAPPY DAYS: ENJOYING THE SPOTLIGHT.

Nurturing a talent for the finer arts, Chrissie eventually quit Akron for a degree course at Kent State University. She studied there during the period of civil unrest, when several unarmed students were gunned down by The National Guard, simply because they'd been protesting against their nation's invasive foreign policy. The incident inspired Neil Young to write 'Ohio' but if it had any marked effect on Chrissie, the world is still awaiting musical proof.

After three years of college drunkenness and debauchery, Chrissie returned to the real world and accepted a job as an illustrator back home in Akron. Employed by a small mail order company, she was expected to design newly-commissioned Coats of Arms, targeted directly at middle-class Americans with more bread than brain cells. She soon took the first in what was to become a long line of waitress jobs.

America's Mid-West had little to offer the ambitious lass, and she knew it. So rather than sit out the rest of her life debating the issue, Chrissie weighed up her options and decided to move to London – and **"start to make things happen."**

On arriving in the capital, one thing happened straight away of course. Chrissie ran out of money. Although she'd checked into one of the city's least salubrious establishments, she soon squandered the 200 greenbacks she'd arrived with. Staring starvation and destitution squarely in the face – and not much liking the look of either – Chrissie got herself a job.

If she'd thought jobs couldn't come much worse than her previous positions of employment, Chrissie couldn't have been more mistaken. This time fate had her selling plastic handbags on a commission only basis, while simultaneously having to cold-shoulder an endless stream of amorous but unwelcome advances. **"I just had to stand there – at this place up towards the corner of Oxford Street – and persuade people that they wanted one of these crummy bags,"** she recalls. **"I don't think I ever sold any!"**

Taking a few other temporary posts, including one with a firm of city architects, Chrissie placed her hopes in the night-life of London. She'd already had her favourite LPs stolen – all Lou Reed and Iggy Pop by this stage – so she figured she had nothing to stay home for anyway.

Partying at every opportunity, Chrissie began to make new acquaintances. One of the first was a young man by the name of Nick Kent – Oxford educated journalist with the *NME*, would-be musician and unquestionably one of the most loquacious and insightful rock writers the UK has ever produced.

Kent's often scathing reviews were a highlight of *NME* throughout the seventies, while his carefully nurtured wasted image – wafer thin, paler than milk and always dressed in ratty black leather – afforded him an air of decadence that, despite his nervous disposition, discouraged any form of confrontation. It was a look that Chrissie herself would soon adopt, albeit with a somewhat healthier pallor. Kent was far more interesting and intelligent than most of the rock stars he interviewed or wrote about, and he and Chrissie soon became lovers.

For some time, Chrissie's home had been a dingy rented flat, barely a bottle's throw from Clapham South's illustrious tube stop. Always in need of a place to stay, Kent moved in for a while and stayed, as they say, a lot longer.

Nick and Chrissie were soon a regular partnership around the London scene, and Chrissie became a welcome and popular guest at the *NME*'s Carnaby Street offices. Never backward in coming forward, the brash American rarely left the

"WHAD'YA MEAN, GO EASY ON THE EYE LINER?" THE DEFIANT POSE.

editorial staff to their work *without* giving them the benefit of her opinions on the current state of contemporary music. Either considerably impressed by her consistent and vociferous remarks – or else justifiably desperate to get rid of her – the paper's assistant editor, Ian McDonald, promptly offered her the opportunity to put her pen where her mouth was. True to form, she accepted.

Chrissie Hynde's first submission as a music journalist appeared in the *NME* on January 19, 1974. The item? . . . a review of Neil Diamond's 'Jonathan Livingston Seagull', hardly the sort of fare that Chrissie would be likely to rush home to play. She described the album as, **"The kind of stuff one whistles while laying in a hammock, clutching a bottle of mescal, and throwing rocks at pelicans."** Which probably meant she couldn't think of much to say about what was essentially a pretentious LP by an artist flushed with an over-abundant sense of his own importance.

Just as she would later write songs with a witty, almost lurid regard for her audience's sexuality, so Ms Hynde would hack out record reviews throughout that winter. Witness if you will her near-iconoclastic retrospective appreciation of The Velvet Underground's 1969 live LP:

"Takes me right back to the teenage years of my virginal innocence, the evening I spent in some dingy hall, eyes fixed on that cat in the striped T-shirt and wrap-around shades, those songs made my eyes water like I was chewing on a wad of aluminium foil, me hoping I could score some dope after the show, me wishing I could be like them . . . The song 'What Goes On' is injected full of characteristic VU sexuality. Reed tosses out the lyrics wet-lipped and oh . . . The audience purses its mouth, the front row thinking, 'I'd like to give him a good . . . ' This sound is what The Velvet Underground was about. This sound is why boys used to pin his picture on their walls way back before they'd admit why."

This *sound* would undoubtedly prove the biggest influence on Chrissie's song-writing career.

By April the would-be musician had grown bored with playing rock critic. She'd also tired of the music scene in general, which is hardly surprising considering the torpid state it had reached in the period immediately prior to the emergence of punk rock. Rock music was now the domain of remote superstars whose lifestyles were far far removed from those of their audience, and the massive stages on which it was performed merely provided a platform for stale rock mannerisms which became more and more conservative as the decade progressed.

There were hitherto uncharted territories that remained unexplored and Chrissie wanted out. In one of her last articles for *NME* she implored that, **"The only way for a new rock consciousness to surface from the dark**

ruins of the Beatle phenomenon, (would be) for some ballsy teen to
step up front and declare war with a defiant 'Move over!'" With The
Sex Pistols still around the corner, could she really have been anticipating their
arrival?

The next thing anyone knew, Chrissie Hynde had done a runner.
"I didn't really know where she'd gone," *NME* editor Nick Logan
later reflected. **"She just disappeared. Quite clearly she knew her own
mind – she was very self assured and very confident. In fact, if I'm
being honest, I'd have to say I'd always found her a bit intimidating
and rather disconcerting."**

Chrissie hadn't spontaneously combusted, she hadn't even burnt out.
She'd simply gone to work at a shop instead. It says a lot about the arrogance
and conceit of music journalists that, in their extraordinarily blinkered view,
the core of contemporary music should be centred around their desk tops.
If Chrissie wasn't seen around the *NME* any more, she must surely be finished
in the business, reasoned her former colleagues.

But Chrissie hadn't even started yet. The shop she'd gone to work at was
the SEX store on London's fashionable Kings Road in Chelsea. Owned by the
husband and wife team of Vivienne Westwood and Malcolm McLaren, it wasn't
so much a clothes emporium, more the embryo for a whole new form of British
youth culture – punk rock. These clothes, which incorporated bondage straps,
PVC and violent imagery, were primarily intended to shock.

Mildly affected by Westwood's interest in SCUM (Society For Cutting-Up
Men) philosophy, and considerably hurt by proven evidence of her boyfriend's
infidelity, Chrissie brought her relationship with Nick Kent to a dramatic and
rather public conclusion and, hoping to ease the pain of separation, went to
Paris to read Kafka. Nick, meanwhile, simply went to pieces.

Ms Hynde had always been attracted to the French way. As a student she'd
been impressed by their painters, their writers. Now she was stunned by their
extraordinary sense of style and *purpose*. The punk movement was just taking
off in Paris (contrary to popular myth, it was not a British invention) at this time
and, although she wasn't in a position to fully participate, she did make enough
musical contacts to permit a more positive return.

Before she did return however, Chrissie would go home to the States
to recharge her batteries. While there, she accepted an offer to sing with a
Cleveland R&B band called Jack Rabbit, and although they weren't the kind of
outfit to go down a storm with the *NME* crew, they provided *exactly* the kind
of experience she needed before launching a musical career in Europe.

Raising the cash from another in her long line of waitressing jobs, Chrissie at
last made it back to Paris, and promptly joined a local band called The Frenchies.
As a singer (she still hadn't started to play guitar in public) it was naturally

important to be able to communicate with her audience. As someone who didn't speak a single word of the language, this proved a trifle tricky. Not surprisingly, she was obliged to quit.

Back in London, Chrissie renewed her friendship with Westwood and McLaren, the latter having lately returned to the capital himself following a stint in the States as manager of the anarchic New York Dolls, whom he had dressed in red and promoted as Communist sympathisers. Whilst there he had been impressed by events occurring down on the Bowery where, at a club called CBGBs, young bands were performing without any of the clichéd mannerisms that current rock wisdom dictated.

In particular he'd spotted one Richard Hell, bass player with a band called Television, who wore his hair spiky and short, his T-shirt torn and his instrument at an angle that clearly indicated he had little experience of playing it. It was an image of vacant abandon, rendered all the more potent because Richard Hell obviously didn't care about what he looked like or what he was playing or what anyone else in the world might think about him.

This trip to New York had renewed his enthusiasm for pop music and Malcolm was looking to launch one or two English versions of these bands. For a while at least, Chrissie Hynde seemed destined to feature in his plans.

"Now I think back," Chrissie thinks back, **"Malcolm tried very hard to get me together with this incredible drummer, Chris Millar, that he'd discovered in Dingwall's one night. Malcolm had *decided* he was a good drummer, even though he'd never actually heard him play, ha-ha! That was Malcolm all over."**

McLaren had a good eye for future stars, for Millar certainly turned out to be the genuine article. As Rat Scabies, he became a founder member of The Damned, the first punk band to release a genuine record and Stiff Records' first signing. Rat, as luck would have it, also recalls the entrepreneur's plans during the period.

"Malcolm was definitely keen to get me together with Chrissie," he reflects, **"and Nick Kent was to rehearse with us as well. I remember they all turned up together one day at this poxy bedsit I had just off Portobello Road. I'd heard of Nick much more than I had of Chrissie – in fact, I was quite impressed that he'd walked into my little room. Chrissie was no one then. I didn't know that she'd written for the *NME*, I just thought she was a loud-mouthed American boiler. Really, she looked the same as she does now."**

Chrissie decided against the liaison, probably because she couldn't see any good coming from a situation which forced her to work with a former boyfriend. Besides which, an alternative was already beginning to rear itself – a role as guitarist in another McLaren outfit, Master Of The Backside!

> CHRISSIE WAS NO ONE THEN . . . I JUST THOUGHT SHE WAS A LOUD-MOUTHED AMERICAN BOILER. REALLY, SHE LOOKED THE SAME AS SHE DOES NOW.

With Rat on drums, a friend of his called Ray Burns (soon to become Captain Sensible) on bass, alongside dual vocalists Dave Vanian and Dave White, the band rehearsed regularly underneath a Paddington fish 'n' chip shop during the latter stages of 1976. They never got around to playing any gigs however, which in retrospect was probably Chrissie's luckiest break to date.

"Malcolm had this weird idea that Chrissie should pretend to be a boy," laughs the Captain a decade later, **"and if we'd ever got around to playing any gigs, part of the act was that she was going to floss us all on-stage, ha-ha!"**

Nice one Malcolm.

Inevitably, the group soon disappeared up its own proverbial. Chrissie wandered off, hoping for pastures new, while her former colleagues formed The Damned. They quickly became stars of course – and Chrissie quickly went back on the scrap-heap.

This situation was becoming all too familiar for the forlorn American. Earlier that year, Chrissie had established a fairly regular working relationship with one Mick Jones. Part colleague, part big-sister figure, the girl from Ohio had helped Mick in his attempts to look more like a 'happening' radical. She'd cut his hair, told him to use his real name (he was calling himself Brady when they first met) and persuaded him to stop dressing like a man obsessed with Mott The Hoople – even though he was!

Having spent the best part of that previous summer rehearsing with Rat Scabies in a line-up called London SS (also featuring Tony and Brian James), Mick was at this stage trying to get a new band together which would be called The Love Boys. If he'd had *his* way, the group would have consisted of himself, Chrissie, Rat, and Nick Kent. Again Hynde's shattered affair with Kent proved the major stumbling block, though Chrissie did agree to participate in another venture – one that McLaren had labelled Big Girls Underwear.

Working within innumerable line-ups of the BGU's, Chrissie became a popular and influential figure around the rehearsal rooms but, as soon as Big Girls Underwear began to make serious headway, Chrissie suddenly wasn't there any more. And by the time they'd evolved into The Clash, Mick Jones was big news – and Chrissie wasn't.

It hadn't been a good year. Friends told her to brighten up, things could be worse. So she brightened up and, the next thing she knew, things were worse . . .

This time it was a problem of a more personal nature however, with her best friend Vivienne Westwood suddenly disowning her for no apparent reason.

"I couldn't quite figure it out at the time," Chrissie says. **"I'd been very good friends with Vivienne and now – at a time I probably**

needed all the friends I'd got – she'd decided I was no longer the right sort of person to know. Apparently she does this kind of thing periodically. But I just went into **SEX** one day, and she suddenly told me to fuck off. I saw her a while later at a gig, at The Roundhouse, and I figured that maybe she'd just been having a down day when I'd seen her before, so I thought I'd go over to her. I was with a load of friends, and I left them and walked across to her. And she just said, 'Ah Chrissie, I thought you were going with the flow . . . and the flow's going that way!' And she pointed in the direction of my friends, who were leaving. So that was that! And, of course, that meant Malcolm wouldn't have anything to do with me either because, what Vivienne said, Malcolm had to go along with."

Quite why Chrissie should have been ostracised in this fashion is hard to say for sure, although it's likely that it had something to do with her increasing association with the flagship of McLaren's empire, The Sex Pistols – and in particular with lead singer Johnny Rotten, the most visible member of the group and soon to become the figurehead for the whole punk movement.

"I saw The Sex Pistols very early indeed, saw lots of their shows," she reflects. **"One of the memorable ones was at the 100 Club. I can remember Johnny Rotten singing 'No Fun', he was sitting on the floor and crying. There were always exciting things like that which made their shows so great. And then there was a horrible fight on-stage and Rotten left – he not only left the stage, he left the club! And Malcolm McLaren went running out into the street to try and retrieve him.**

IN PRAISE OF HEREFORD.

IN PRAISE OF BACKING BANDS.

"Meanwhile, on-stage, the band were so frustrated. Steve Jones couldn't handle it, and he ripped his guitar strings off with one hand. So then Rotten finally came back in, and when he realised that Steve had ripped the strings off his guitar and couldn't play any more, Rotten leapt back on-stage and went, 'Okay, what's next!' This is 15 minutes since he'd left. So it looked like it was Steve's fault they couldn't carry on. Rotten was horrible and would always make anyone else look bad if he possibly could. And while they were playing, he kept picking up his mike stand, over his shoulder, trying to spear Glen Matlock. There was always this tension that he was trying to do grievous bodily harm to Matlock on stage .

". . . Anyway, I'm sure that Vivienne and Malcolm's sudden change of heart towards me had something to do with me starting to teach John (Rotten/Lydon) how to play the guitar. He wasn't supposed to know anything outside of what The Pistols were doing directly – even though the group all clearly hated each other. Anyway, John really wanted to play the guitar, if only so he'd have a better idea of what the group were doing. So he used to come over to my place in Clapham, and I taught him a few chords. I can remember now, meeting him on Clapham Common, sitting there looking all lost with his acoustic guitar . . . Malcolm or Vivienne obviously got to hear about it though!"

BACK ON THE CHAIN GANG: THE PRETENDERS HIT THE ROAD – AND THE BIG TIME.

Following a brief liaison with the Croydon based Johnny Moped band – **"I knew I had no place standing next to such a charismatic figure,"** Chrissie jokes. **"So I gracefully left when he threw me out!"** – and an even briefer romantic fling with muso-turned producer Nick Lowe, Chrissie finally got a break when Chris Spedding offered her the chance to sing backing vocals on an album he was cutting in London. The record was entitled 'Hurt', and represents Chrissie's first involvement with producer Chris Thomas – who would later work with The Pretenders.

Spedding, one of the most respected session musicians of his generation, had originally met Chrissie during her stint in Paris, and didn't quite understand why her career was still on the launching pad during these, the spring months of 1977.

"Though she was always trying to form a group," says Spedding, **"nothing really seemed to happen for her. She was clearly having a difficult time. For a while she'd be telling you how she'd just started to play with someone, and then the next time you saw her, it would turn out she'd been fired . . . In fact, her whole involvement with the punk scene was quite interesting in retrospect. For although she was certainly one of its instigators, Chrissie always seemed too much of an individual, too much of a *rebel* in fact, to ever get totally into it!"**

If she had a cause, Chrissie was more preoccupied with her personal situation to let it show. Instead, the rebel without a flat busied herself searching for somewhere to live. A series of squats seemed to present the easiest answer.

"I lived in a whole load of those places," she remembers, **"with no hot water or bathroom, or anything. They tended to be pretty tidy though. There was a guy in one place who made a bit of a mess – but he got thrown out. He said, 'I can stay if I want, this is a squat!' And the guy throwing him out said, 'No you can't, because *you're* an asshole and *I'm* bigger than you!' Ha-ha. And that was the end of that. I had a little tiny lock on the door of that place, and that's the one you used to see around Sid Vicious' neck. I gave it to him."

Eventually Chrissie ended up in a Hells Angel squat (also frequented by Lemmy) and, rather fortuitously for her, fell in with pop maverick Tony Secunda. A one-time manager of The Move and Steeleye Span, Secunda was trying to build a stable of stars on the back of the punk movement and seemed happy to take Lemmy's Motorhead – along with Chrissie – under his wing until they cracked it.

Secunda paid them each £20 a week which, although it might not sound a lot today, seemed like a fortune to the destitute American at the time. More importantly than the cash however, her new-found manager was also able to provide a much more positive vibe than she'd previously been used to. And when the time came to lay down the all-important demo, Secunda was there to pay the bills.

Singing and playing guitar *together* for the first time now, Chrissie phoned bassist Fred Berk, an ally from Johnny Moped's outfit, and invited him to come and join her. Meanwhile Secunda supplied a drummer in the unlikely shape of Nigel Pegrum, percussionist with the manager's successful folk troupe Steeleye Span!

"We recorded four numbers up at Milner Sound, an eight-track studio just off the Kings Road," remembers Pegrum, **"and they were all bloody good . . . 'The Phonecall' was one of them if I remember right. It was clear straight away that Chrissie was in charge – she had a very strong idea of how her songs should sound. They relied very much on her feel for rhythm, as they'd all been written on the guitar. In fact, she was well on the way to becoming a very competent musician.**

"As soon as I sat down at the drums though, and tried to play a simple 4/4 beat, it all became very awkward. Her writing, or so it transpired, was not within the conventions of time signatures, often because of the controlling influence of her lyrics. More often than not, she had to add another bar onto the end of a line, simply because she'd decided to tag on another word!

"Four months after those demos, Chrissie called me up and asked me to join the band that ended up being The Pretenders. However, Steeleye Span had just split up, leaving something of a sour taste in my mouth about groups and, to my great regret, I declined the offer."

Sadly Secunda and Chrissie later fell-out and, although her next manager (an old friend from Ohio whose name has been lost to posterity) liked the demo tape, he had no experience in the industry, and soon ran out of money. What he *did* manage to do before making his getaway however, was line-up an appointment for Chrissie to visit Anchor Records' A&R man, Dave Hill.

Hynde's face wasn't new to Hill. He'd seen her a hundred times before in one seedy rock club or another. **"I used to think she was really interesting to look at,"** he later claimed. **"There was certainly something very attractive about her. Also, she seemed a bit weird."**

As luck would have it, Dave Hill liked his pop stars a bit on the weird side and, since he was in the process of setting up a new label called Real Records, he invited Chrissie to be its first signing. Ms Hynde didn't have much on that week, so she accepted.

Set to work down a dingy basement in Covent Garden, Chrissie rehearsed with an endless stream of musicians throughout the winter of 1978, only taking time out to supply backing vocals for Mick Farren's LP of the period, 'Vampires Stole My Lunch Money'. Farren, himself a journalist-turned musician, remembers well the renewed vigour she seemed to have in the studio during this time. **"Chrissie seemed especially pleased to be harmonising alongside Sonja Kristina (former singer with Curved Air, who was now living with her drummer boyfriend Stewart Copeland, a member of a newly-formed but little known trio, The Police), and if it hadn't been for the presence of another woman, she may well have buggered off halfway through the session. It wouldn't have been out of character.**

"HOW'S THIS FOR MICK JAGGER?"

"WELL, WHAT ABOUT MY PRINCESS ANNE THEN?"

"Instead though, she stayed, and was very noisy and very extrovert about the fact that she wanted to be a rock 'n' roll star. To be fair, Chrissie had always seemed very determined, and she was always strumming away to records – in fact, her strumming along to records could become a complete pain.

"At the same time however, there were definitely extreme doubts whether she would ever actually get it together. She always seemed in a state of panic, always flying off at tangents, like a yoyo with the string about to be cut. She was *always* very twitchy."

Twitchy or not, Chrissie was once again in the starting stalls and, guessing it might be the last chance to prove herself, seemed to be making a conscious effort to give it her best shot.

First though, she'd need the right kind of band. A studio drummer, Gas Wild, seemed to show promise, and he also claimed to know a bass player who might do a turn in rehearsal. His name was Pete Farndon, an old acquaintance from Hereford.

"Hereford?" Chrissie is reported to have said at the time, **"What the *fuck's* Hereford!?!"**

CHAPTER TWO

The Hereford Connection

LOCAL HEROES: PETE AND MARTIN SHARE A JOKE.

Hereford is an attractive medieval city built on the banks of the River Wye close to the Welsh border in the county now known as Hereford and Worcester. With a modern-day population of around 50,000, it is known largely for its agricultural tradition and as a centre for the manufacture of cider. Its only connection with rock 'n' pop is as the birthplace for four fifths of Mott The Hoople who quit the town for London where they hooked up with Ian Hunter and went on to fame and modest fortune – but none of that's important right now.

What *is* important is that the day Gas Wild telephoned Pete Farndon's parents' house, their restless bass playing son was not only at home, but also more than ready to move back to the capital for one last crack at the big-time.

Born in Hereford in 1953 and expelled from public school at 15, Pete Farndon's first musical adventure was with an outfit called Cold River Lady.

This band enjoyed solid local success and eventually made the move to London where they hoped to gain record company recognition.

The breakthrough wasn't to be however, so Pete quit the group, got himself a flat in Clapham, and started hanging-out around the new, fast-rising punk venues of the period. Pete was greatly impressed by the high-energy sound of the London club scene, and was just about to get his own band together when, quite by chance, he was offered a gig with an Australian folk combo called The Bushwackers. Yes *really*!

With nothing much better to do with his time and talents, he accepted an invitation to travel the world with his newly acquired antipodean pals, and duly set off on a trek which would exhaust the best part of a year. Ending up down-under however, the bassist suddenly decided the culture shock was too much and, with the bright lights of Hereford still beckoning, high-tailed it back home via a drug binge in Hong Kong.

Soon refreshed, Pete's musical ambitions were undecided and, walking a tightrope between 'carrying-on' and 'packing-it-in', looked on his old friend's call as something of a life-saver. Ironically, it was probably the chance he'd been waiting for.

Back in the big smoke then, Farndon soon arranged to meet Chrissie Hynde in a pub on Portobello Road. And although a year later he couldn't recall the name of the pub, he would never forget his first impressions of the leather-clad Ms Hynde.

"I walked into this boozer," he reflected, **"and there was this American with a big mouth across the other side of the bar. She said 'Hi', and then turned around and ignored me for about an hour. I thought, am I really gonna be in a band with this cunt?!**

"As soon as we got down to her rehearsal room though – which was the scummiest basement I've ever been in in my life – I began to look at her a little differently. The first thing we played was 'Groove Me' by King Floyd. The second thing we played was this great country and western song of hers called 'Tequila'. I was looking at this woman like, you know – fuck man, I'll never forget it. We go in, we do a soul number, we do a country and western number, and then we did 'The Phonecall' which is like the heaviest fuckin' punk rocker you could do in 5/4 time. Impressed? I was very impressed!"

Impressed enough to join forces in fact. Pete quickly established himself in a room in Tufnell Park, and took over responsibility for the arrangements of Chrissie's oddly structured songs. Within weeks they'd become lovers, and Wild – the man who'd brought them together – was out on his ear.

Rehearsing in an Endell Street basement – downstairs from Eddie Ryan's drumstore in fact – there shouldn't have been much difficulty in finding an

FARNDON WITH MEAN-MACHINE AND WITH L-R, CHAMBERS, HYNDE AND HONEYMAN-SCOTT.

adequate drummer to work with. But Chrissie was getting particular in her old age, and the only one she could get excited about was Motorhead's Phil (Philthy Animal) Taylor.

"His group were really going through the doldrums at that time," Pete later explained. **"In fact, it didn't look as though they had any future at all. So round about July of '78, me and Chrissie came up with this awfully dubious plan. We wanted to try to pirate Philthy Animal over to us, or at least let him know he was welcome to join us if he wanted to –** *without* **actually saying 'leave Motorhead'.**

"So we told him that we were auditioning a guitarist, and just needed a drummer for the session. Then we had to come up with a reasonable guitarist to make the whole thing seem credible. And eventually I decided on this little bloke from Hereford I'd known for a long time – whose sister I used to knock off – called Jimmy Honeyman-Scott. He was working in a local music store in my home town at the time. He'd actually given up playing, except for occasional local R&B bands. He had a girlfriend, and a flat next to my old school. I got in touch with him by telegram, and asked if he'd come up to London for the weekend. We paid him £100 and a load of speed.

"We played with Phil for a weekend without stopping, but the drummer wasn't totally convinced. Besides which, he was still really loyal to Motorhead. But Chrissie and I were *very* **impressed by Jimmy!"**

James Honeyman-Scott, born in Hereford in 1957, was always a natural obsessive. He'd fallen in love with rock 'n' roll at the age of four, when he first heard The Shadows on the wireless. His love affair with the guitar began days later when an older brother introduced him to a friend who had a big red guitar. **"Nothing ever impressed me more than that,"** Jimmy would later recall. **"Nothing that is, except possibly seeing Rockpile play for the first time . . .**

"When I was young I actually thought you needed a licence to play the guitar! I thought you had to be 17 to play guitar legally. I can remember thinking of nothing else. At school we were asked to write an essay and, at the age of six, I wrote mine on guitars, amps the lot. In high school they wanted an essay on any object you were completely familiar with, so I wrote an entire essay on guitars – right down to the screwheads."

Jimmy got his own guitar when he was 10. The first song? 'House Of The Rising Sun' – the Dylan version. A love of folk-inspired work quickly developed into an adoration of west coast music, most specifically Brian Wilson's surf anthems recorded by The Beach Boys, as well as a later obsession for both Eric Clapton and Peter Green's Fleetwood Mac.

By comparison, school held little fascination for the budding muso. So when the opportunity of expulsion arrived at the age of 15, Jimmy left an already broken home to seek solace as a roadie. By the time he was 16 however, the young guitarist was already playing on a semi-professional basis with one of the seventies' lesser known curiosities, an outfit named The Enid.

Jimmy couldn't keep away from Hereford for long however, and on his return in 1974, he promptly joined a local band called Cheeks. Formed by Verden Allen, one-time keyboard player with Mott The Hoople, the group always looked like signing a deal but, for one reason or another, never did. After three years of anticipatory let-downs, Jimmy left the Cheeks in favour of a job with a local guitar shop.

THE PRETENDERS IN THEIR ELEMENT: IN FRONT OF A LIVE AUDIENCE.

Increasingly dependent on amphetamines during this time, it's worth stressing that, contrary to popular myth, The Pretenders were not responsible for turning Honeyman-Scott into a junkie. Indeed, by his own admission, Jimmy's drug obsession had set in long before he met Ms Hynde.

"In actual fact, The Pretenders saved my life," Jimmy told reporters shortly after his swift rise to fame. **"Before I joined the group, I was eight-and-a-half stone. Now I'm 10-and-a-half. I was treated for erosion of the stomach . . . It was pathetic how bad I was. I was selling everything. I'd do anything to score a quarter of a gram. In Hereford there was nothing to do except get wasted."**

Out of necessity however, Jimmy found something else to do. Packing in the dead end retailing career, he got himself a job as a gardener. For the first time in years, he was able to tune into popular radio all day, totally undisturbed, and actually *listen* to the sounds that were selling. For a man who'd been totally unmoved by the punk explosion, even Radio One became an education.

"It's funny how things work out," Jimmy later recalled. **"I can remember I had the radio on while I was digging in this garden and, all of a sudden, 'So It Goes' by Nick Lowe came on. I thought he'd ripped my guitar sound off. Then they played a song by Elvis Costello. All of a sudden this guy Nick Lowe changed my whole life. Finally there was a light at the end of the tunnel. I got my guitar out of the cupboard, dusted off the strings and stopped gardening. I began to rip off what Nick had ripped off, only adding more to it."**

Although pleased to be called to London, Jimmy wasn't immediately struck by Farndon's set-up with 'the Yank', and was in no mood to discard his comfy home existence (he was engaged by now) in favour of sleepless nights on north London floorboards. The drugs he could earn in rehearsal time however, would prove another matter altogether!

With the guitarist's fees invariably being paid through one drug currency or another, a temporary routine was quickly established. Hynde and Farndon worked on the songs, Honeyman-Scott would come down to rehearse them, while a series of drummers would be auditioned and then dropped.

Although Jimmy had carefully avoided any impression of long-term intent, Chrissie and Pete secretly hoped to be able to persuade him to join up. With an album's worth of material just about ready, they didn't fancy having to wait around while another guitarist could be found. So when they finally built a working relationship with drummer Gerry Mackleduff, Chrissie decided to go for broke.

Booking Regents Park Studio for a whole weekend in July 1978, the four-piece recorded 'I Can't Control Myself', 'Precious', 'The Phonecall', 'Stop Your Sobbing', along with that country number, 'Tequila'. While the other three sat around congratulating themselves on a job well done, the driving force was on the phone trying to persuade Nick Lowe to produce something from the session.

Lowe, nicknamed 'Basher' for having more than occasionally requested musicians to 'bash it out' while producing them, was enjoying a second career with the advent of punk. His first was as bassist with Brinsley Schwartz, erstwhile pub-rockers before rocking in pubs became a musical genre of its own, but the Brinsleys, though much loved by a small band of aficionados, could never overcome charges of hype that followed their extraordinary New York launch by manager Dave Robinson.

More recently Robinson had teamed up with Jake Riviera, aka Andrew Jakeman, a former tour manager for Dr Feelgood and soon to become manager of Elvis Costello, to launch Stiff Records, the liveliest independent label to pick up on the London punk/new wave movement. Lowe, as well as playing bass with the Riviera managed Rockpile and recording some promising solo material, was now unofficial house producer for Stiff.

"I'll never forget it," chuckles Nick. **"Chrissie just rang me up out of the blue, and said she wanted me to listen to these demos. Thinking about what her songs used to be like when I knew her before, I wasn't all that keen. Also she said, 'I've got this band together.' Just what the world needed, I thought, another band.**

"But she just kept on and on phoning me up at all hours! She said, 'You don't have to listen to the whole tape – just listen to this one song that I've got, a Kinks number called 'Stop Your Sobbing', you'll really like it.' So I thought . . . put her off!

. . . . JUST ANOTHER PARTY.

"I was saying, 'Well yeah, let's get together sometime . . . ' And suddenly she says, 'Look, I'm in the phone box at the end of your road, can I come round?' I couldn't put it off any longer. So Chrissie arrived a couple of minutes later, and I told her, 'The thing is, I've one rule here – which is that I never listen to anyone's cassette if they're in the same room. It's too embarrassing – if it stinks, I find it very hard to say what I really mean.' Quite honestly, I'd rather lie. But she agreed, and went off for a walk around the block.

"I put on 'Stop Your Sobbing', and I thought the way they'd done it was *hideous*! **But on the other hand her voice was** *fantastic*! **It was totally different from how she was singing when I first knew her. Then it was more that Janis Joplin-stroke-Maggie Bell squawk that I always find grossly offensive, yet which so many girl singers seem to choose – unless they go for the other choice, which is the hearts and flowers, floor length dresses stuff."**

Lowe and Hynde had first rubbed shoulders, among other things, during the latter's spell with the *NME*. At that time, Nick was still playing with the Brinsleys, so his rapid rise to prominence must be seen as testimony to a good ear for a winning sound. And he *did* like Chrissie's voice.

"In fact, it was just what I was after!" he asserts. **"I was looking to find a girl singer who sounded like the sort of girls you see working in Woolworths or Boots. Some of those chicks you see working on the checkout counter look so great – tough but, well, feminine as well. There were a few of them in the sixties – Sandie Shaw, who Chrissie later got compared with, and Leslie Gore as well. They had a good bellow, even if it was a bit dodgy on the pitching. It still sounded sexy as hell! So, er, I went sprinting down the road after her."**

Chrissie now had her bargaining power and, as Jimmy Honeyman-Scott would later recall, she didn't wait to use it. **"Listen, I don't know whether or not you want to join our group full-time,"** she told the guitarist, **"but we've got Nick Lowe producing our first single!"** Chrissie thought that should swing it, and she was right. She now had a deal *and* a band.

For the first time in her life, Chrissie finally seemed keen to exploit an opportunity. The only stumbling block would be other people's schedules.

The bad news was that Lowe was already booked to work on someone else's material at East Acton's Eden Studios. The good news, though, was that said material turned out to be Elvis Costello's 'Armed Forces' album. Gracious as ever, the singer-songwriter gladly offered the newcomers some free time before he started – and whether this was because Elvis wasn't yet ready to use the studio himself, or whether he's just a very gracious chap anyway – no one stopped to ponder. **"I told Chrissie we'd have to be quick about it,"** remembers Lowe. **"And that the whole group would just have to do what I said. There wasn't time to busk about!"**

The song, 'Stop Your Sobbing', turned out well. Everything sounded exactly the way Lowe imagined it might, and the musicians were delighted with the direction that his experience had been able to provide. It's all the more ironic then, that the finishing touch should actually have been the result of a complete accident.

ONCE MORE WITH FEELING.

"It came about when Jimmy started fiddling with the controls," said Lowe years later. "By accident, I then pushed a button which resulted in that long echo thing at the end, where the voice sings a line, and then there's a delay echo on it. People thought that Chrissie had sung the lines twice but, in fact, there's just one vocal with a very long delay on it. The delay is *so* long that, so it would be in time, we had to use a special machine on which the spools hardly turned at all. It worked a treat. The song had real charm, and it was done so quickly."

The B-side however, was done even quicker. "In the days when I was part of an EMI mud-on-the-wall group," laughs Lowe, "we used to go into the studio at nine o'clock in the morning until noon. We had two-and-a-half hours to do the A-side, and half-an-hour for the B-side. The old man who was producing would say, 'Right fellers, you can stay or you can go, but you don't come anywhere near this desk, and you don't talk.' Ha-ha! It was just like that with this lot. I said, 'Come on, let's do the B-side, let's do 'The Wait'. Let's bang it out.' And really I didn't like the song at all. But funnily enough, after the passage of time, I actually started preferring it to 'Stop Your Sobbing'. In the end I thought it was great."

Although Chrissie did ask him to work on some more of the band's material, Nick Lowe never got around to it. "I can't remember why I didn't," he now wonders, "I suppose it was probably out of prejudice. I honestly didn't think the group was as good as it later turned out to be. I was really off the *rama-lama* punk thing at the time, and I s'pose I thought that was the way Chrissie was going to go – which was really unfair, 'cos I'd never seen the group play live, or even heard any of the other stuff she'd been writing. In fact, I simply didn't realise that Chrissie could write such good songs. To think I turned them down . . . I've worn sackcloth and ashes ever since I made that decision."

One step away from the big-time, sleepless nights on north London floorboards no longer seemed like such a problem, so Jimmy now welcomed the invitation to join Chrissie and Pete in the latter's increasingly cramped abode. The move to London hadn't been quite as traumatic as he'd imagined it would be, mainly because he hadn't had to sever *all* his ties with Hereford. For not only was Farndon an old acquaintance, but Jimmy had also discovered another old pal, one Martin Chambers, who'd actually taken up residence just around the corner in Tufnell Park.

Drummer with Honeyman-Scott's former group Cheeks, Chambers, born in 1952 and another alumnus of the Hereford school of rock 'n' roll, had actually been on Farndon's list of 'drummers to call' during the period they'd been auditioning for the hot seat. His last known employment *had* been with another Hereford based band, The Dave Stewart Sound. Unfortunately though they hadn't been able to track him down at the time, mainly – as it turns out – because he'd run off to pursue a career as a driving instructor with the British School Of Motoring in Baker Street! Now working as a musical 'temp' through the classified ads in *Melody Maker*, Chambers had stories to share, and who better to share them with than his old Hereford chums and their newly acquired American friend. It soon became clear that, socially at least, the quartet would get on famously. Professionally however, any decision would have to be postponed while more pressing matters were sorted out.

So what could be more pressing than the line-up of the group? Simple – the stability of the record company, that's what!

While Chrissie and the band were busying themselves rehearsing and recording, their label's parent company, Anchor Records, had experienced a serious bout of financial problems – the result of which meant that the group's label, Real, would eventually be taken over by the massive WEA conglomerate.

This would probably prove the band's best break to date. In many cases monetary problems can wreck a band's career but for Chrissie's group the prevailing winds couldn't have blown harder in their favour. With Anchor boss Ian Ralfini giving them the highest possible recommendation in passing them over, WEA chairman John Fruin would soon be making them a priority act.

Not destined to become the band's manager until the following year, Dave Hill *was* still in charge of the Real label however, and it was in this capacity that he booked the line-up's first ever gig. In August, 1978, they played in the small Yorkshire town of Wakefield – as support act to their label-mates Strangeways.

An October trip to France followed, where the still unnamed band played a week's residency at The Gibus Club in Paris. Billed as The Chrissie Hynde Group, the girl herself changed the venue's poster so it read Dinosaur Eating Cars, a term Nick Lowe had used to describe the ideal kind of drum sound required in post-punk pop – a sound Gerry Mackleduff was reportedly having trouble trying to recreate.

Back in London there were dirty deeds to be done, and Pete was the man who took responsibility. **"Behind Gerry's back, I got Martin to come down to our rehearsal place,"** Farndon later confessed. **"And just the two of us played together. We went through all the odd time signatures, and he seemed to be able to manage them all. Then I got Chrissie and Jimmy to come down, and it sounded fuckin' great.**

"At this stage Gerry still hadn't said that he *definitely* wanted in on the band. Basically I saw this as giving us the option of throwing him out and getting Martin in. Martin had the same sense of humour

NICK LOWE: AN INSPIRATION.

CHRISSIE FOLLOWING JIMMY'S LEAD – IN MORE WAYS THAN ONE.

as Jimmy and I, and it really saves a lot of trouble if everybody knows each other. And about 10 days before it was time to do the photo for the cover of the 'Sobbing' single, it became apparent that Gerry was going to be the odd one out. It was agreed the night before the photo session, that Martin should join the band.

"I was probably being a bit ruthless at the time, but I really wanted the band to do well. Even so, I'll never forget having to do what was one of the worst things I've ever done in my life . . . I went round to Gerry Mackleduff's to pick him up to take him to the studio, as he thought. He said, 'I'll be with you in a minute, I'm just putting my coat on' – and I had to say, 'Gerry, you're not coming, you're not in the band.' He just said, 'Oh well, fair enough' and we came to a financial arrangement, which was absolutely nothing when you consider how big the band became. We gave him £200 and a lump of hash.

"As for Martin, well he was already waiting for us in the pub round the corner from the photographer's studio . . . having a quick haircut!"

In view of the fact it took a photo session to push them into finalising their line-up, it comes as little surprise to discover their moniker also sprung to the fore at the eleventh hour. Indeed, the very day before their début single was to be pressed, a name for the band still had to be established.

In order to reach a final decision then, Pete, Chrissie and a friend called Vermilion all gathered round at Joy Farren's (Mick's former wife) flat in order to thrash about a few ideas. Typically no one remembers who said it first, but someone in the room came up with the song title, 'The Great Pretender'.

"That was it," reported Pete, "I immediately rushed to Joy's telephone and called Dave Hill. 'What about The Pretenders?' He said he liked it . . . simple as that!"

CHAPTER THREE

Live And Let Die

MARTIN CHAMBERS: IN THE HOTTEST SEAT IN TOWN.

Complete with new drummer, The Pretenders performed their first live show together on December 1, 1978, at the Nashville in West London. Playing second fiddle to the headlining act, Racing Cars, their set mightn't have attracted the attention it deserved, but this would not prove to be a lasting problem. A month later 'Stop Your Sobbing' was finally unleashed and, all of a sudden, The Pretenders were the talk of the town, so to speak.

The critics loved the single, even the one employed by *Melody Maker*, who got really carried away with the adjectival possibilities. 'Astute' and 'attractive' were the ones finally utilised, an interesting combination from a journal no longer appreciative of either term.

But the *Melody Maker* was the underdog in a grisly circulation war at the time, and was no doubt as desperate to champion a new band with potential as the *NME* were to champion anything at all – so long as they got there before their rivals. Slow off the mark to appreciate the significance of punk, *MM* had lost considerable ground to *NME* recently and the increased circulation it enjoyed during the early seventies had been almost entirely eroded away.

As it happened they both got there at the same time, so when the night came for the band to play their first ever headlining gig – at West Hampstead's Moonlight Club upstairs in the Railway Hotel – the audience was jam-packed with journalists, envious rival A&R people and many other scene-setters of indeterminate function, all demanding to be impressed.

"It was crazy," recalls Chrissie. **"We thought it would start off really low-key but, instead, I seemed to know just about every person in the audience . . . And of course everyone was trying to be really tactful, because they'd just heard that Sid Vicious had died in the States, and they knew I knew him, so didn't want to upset me before I went on-stage. Then about five seconds before we went on, someone just turned to me and said, 'Hey, Sid's dead!' Great . . . "**

The news didn't seem to affect her performance, and the critics continued to be encouraged. Indeed, with every show, reports escalated as to the future possibilities for the group.

With genuine concern that they shouldn't receive destructive adoration before their time, yet simultaneously appreciative of how the outfit could have caused such a buzz in the first place, Nick Kent soon proffered a telling review of his former lover's band in *NME*.

"LOOK, NO HANDS!" JIMMY DEMONSTRATES HIS LATEST TRICK.

"THE FIRST ONE TO GRIN LOSES 10 TEAM POINTS." THE PRETENDERS PLAY GAMES.

"Five gigs played and the vultures are already congregating," he snarled, **"ready to sweep and shower the superlatives down on The Pretenders like so much bird shit. Any possible natural progression could well be stymied by the demands for mercurial leaps and bloated expectations that'll doubtless cause serious friction unless this whole premature circus is held in check by the enterprise itself, and those media folk in the responsible positions (though they seldom, if ever, admit to it) let nature take its course . . . "**

Clearly supportive though, Kent continued: **"As a dance band there's simply no one to touch The Pretenders right now . . . Perhaps most exciting are Hynde's own songs . . . The goods are delivered with an uncanny adeptness, the potential seems positively limitless and, yes, there's not a new band around that can measure up to their shadow!"**

Kent may not have believed his concerns could ever become reality and that a media inspired change of fortune would befall the group or, for that matter, their record label. But if this was the case, then he'd seriously underestimated their intelligence. Dave Hill was definitely a worried man!

"There we were on our first couple of gigs," explains Hill, **"and everybody was running around saying that** *this* **was the peak of the group, that** *this* **was the time to see them – that it was** *now* **that we were firing on all 10 cylinders . . . And the truth of the matter was that we weren't. There's no doubt we could really have come a cropper after that kind of attention coming so early. It's so often the same, something good comes along and everybody rushes in because they want to be first. It might be good for the papers, but it isn't always good for the band."**

Strangely, 'Stop Your Sobbing' only reached 32 in the charts, but with a string of club dates maintaining the group's profile, Hill was forced to refuse many more interviews until his charges had something new to discuss. A few more songs seemed like a good place to start, so the search for a producer began in earnest.

Since The Pretenders were playing a handful of spring dates at London's prestigious Marquee Club, Hill ensured that Chris Thomas would attend at least one of the shows. Thomas, who up till then had been famed for the diversity of his work with such artists as The Sex Pistols, Pink Floyd, Roxy Music and Paul McCartney, remembers being pleasantly surprised by the potential of The Pretenders.

"I was immediately struck by the songs," says Chris. **"I thought they showed an incredibly varied range . . . although, to be honest, I did feel they were a little flat as a stage band. The *performance* was actually very monotonous, with all the guitars and amps turned full up to 10. Real switch-the-hoover-on, very typical post-punk stuff. I remember they finished with Love Sculpture's 'Sabre Dance'.**

"But I thought the possibilities *within* the songs were quite immense. I especially liked the 'Brass In Pocket' number, so I went backstage afterwards and told Chrissie so. However, Chrissie told me she didn't really like 'Brass In Pocket'. I insisted it was going to be a hit though, and I told her if she wasn't going to record it, she should send it over to Willie Mitchell and it would make her a fortune!

"Anyway, I told her I was totally knackered after working on Wings' 'Back To The Egg' album. I didn't want to go straight in to make another LP, and have the record company breathing down my neck to deliver it to them. Yet equally I knew Chrissie was great and I really liked her songs. So what she suggested was that we do some very casual recording without worrying about what the consequences of it would be. After about a month 'Kid' came along, we recorded it, but then I was committed to go off and work with Pete Townshend on his 'Empty Glass' album. So that was that for the time being."

This presented few problems for the band. Promptly releasing the new song, and then running round the country trying to promote it, their schedule actually coincided perfectly with that of the producer.

'Kid', which featured a rhythmic yet gloriously melodic Beatlesque guitar solo from Honeyman-Scott, was another critical success. Backed-with 'Tattooed Love Boys', it was described as 'effortlessly elegant' by the *NME*, while rivals *Melody Maker* revealed it to be a 'double-sided scorcher'. . . yeeees. Curiously though, the record barely did better than their first release – this one only climbing to 31 in the charts, before finally disappearing without trace. What was the matter? Didn't the record-buying public know that it'd been officially deemed a 'scorcher'? Or did *Melody Maker* weigh-in with as little impact in the seventies as it clearly does today?!

Either way, the promotional trek didn't do the group's stage show any harm at all and, when the summer finally came to a close, The Pretenders had at least got closer to playing together as a group.

Back in Islington's Wessex Studios, they and Chris Thomas began to slog away on what would become the début album. 'Slog' being the operative word, as Pete Farndon would later reveal.

"We really were recording for a long time," he remembers. **"Chris Thomas was painstakingly meticulous. Also, he wanted everyone to be there all the time. It was never a case of, 'Oh, you've done your bit, you can go home now.' The only exception to that was that Chrissie would never have anyone in the studio while she was recording her vocals – not even members of the group could be present! The atmosphere was always really heavy."**

As time progressed, and the album didn't, it became increasingly obvious that the material was unlikely to be ready for the planned pre-Christmas release date, and that The Pretenders' LP wouldn't actually see light of day until the following year, 1980. Though far from ignorant of the need to keep to deadlines, Chrissie was determined not to allow record company pressure to undermine the recording process, and consequently rejected any requests to speed up proceedings.

FARNDON'S 'SILLY HAT' PHASE.

Time would prove their patience to have been a virtue, and when Chris Thomas' choice for the third single, 'Brass In Pocket', was eventually released ahead of the album, the record-buying public responded even more enthusiastically than the band could have hoped. The single finally made it to the top of the singles chart on January 19, 1980 and, although Chrissie never liked the song herself, she nonetheless accepted that the producer's finger was probably closer to the pulse of public opinion than even she'd previously believed.

"I hated 'Brass In Pocket' with a vengeance," Chrissie claims. **"It was a phenomenon that evades me completely. I was honestly very disappointed it was such a big hit, and I was very embarrassed by it. Fuckin' Ada! I hated it so much that, if I was in Woolworths and they started playing it, then I'd have to run out of the store . . . I mean, what do you do though? Everyone connected with you – the guys in the group, the manager, the producer, the record company – they're all saying, 'This is a fantastic song, this is a number one record.' And I'm going, 'Well that's exactly the reason why *I* don't like it, it's so obvious!'**

"When Chris Thomas was mixing it, I kept saying to him, 'Chris, mix my vocals down will you, please?' And he would just refuse. 'No they have to be like this, they're meant to be clear – so people can hear them!' And obviously Chris was right because, when it was played on the radio, what you heard were the lyrics. But I still hated the fuckin' thing."

As the excitement of playing their first headlining gig together was numbed by the death of Chrissie's former pal Sid Vicious, so The Pretenders victorious appearance on BBC's *Top Of The Pops* would be marred by another tragedy, the death of a new flatmate, Kevin Sparrow.

Her relationship with Pete Farndon becoming strained, Chrissie had moved out of the bass player's north London room, and into a Covent Garden slum inhabited by Sparrow. Sadly though, the friendship would never be cemented since Sparrow was soon to die of a heroin overdose – on Christmas Day in fact. Irony of ironies, the young man's funeral turned out to be the same day that Chrissie's band were due to record their first TV appearance as chart-toppers.

Chrissie fought back the tears alright, but the tensions of her private life were already beginning to stain her personality – almost to the point where she became impossible to work with.

"She could certainly be very difficult," reckoned Pete. **"She would always want her own way without listening to what anybody else had to say. And it was tense enough when we would go on the road and try to produce our studio sound on-stage. Nobody in the band had**

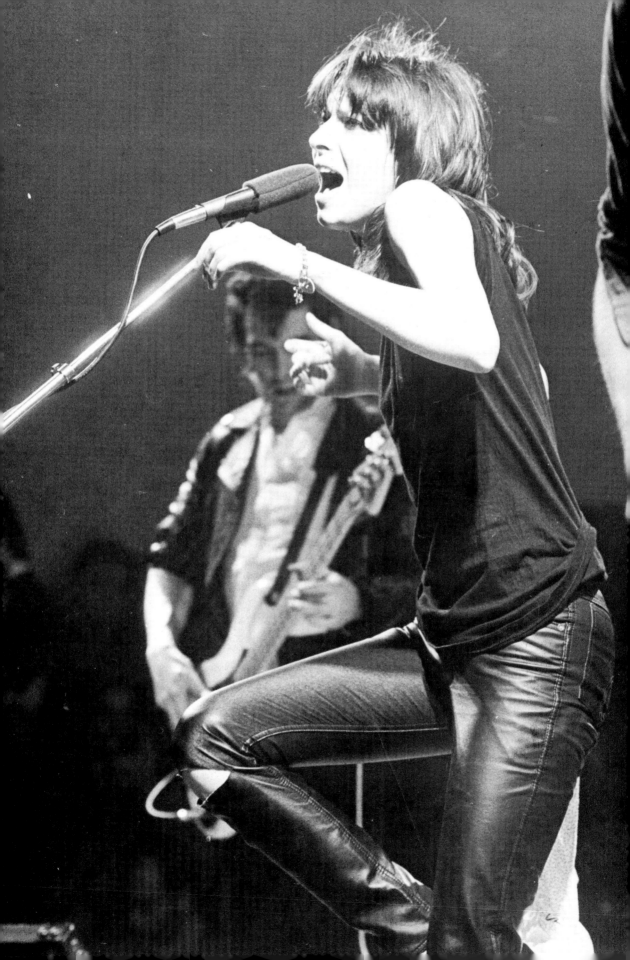

ever really been in a working outfit before. Experience really comes into getting up on-stage and performing. At first, Chrissie had no idea how to turn it on on-stage. Also, she *never* wanted to tour.

"She and I started to fall apart really because there was such an awful lot of pressure to cope with. To actually keep a relationship going *and* work together in those situations was very, very difficult."

The stress and strains of life in the fast lane did take a back seat for a few days however, as the band allowed themselves the luxury of enjoying their current success. For no sooner had 'Brass In Pocket' struck gold in the singles chart, than the band's eponymously titled LP went straight into the albums chart at number one. No one could quite believe it. Which was understandable really, since it *was* fairly unbelievable.

Rumours of hyping soon begot allegations of hyping, and WEA, who had only recently been exposed in a *World In Action* TV special, found themselves in a tangle that even Houdini wouldn't have relished.

While everyone on the sidelines blushed a subtle shade of beetroot, the woman at the centre of the controversy calmly accepted the likelihood that underhand tactics had been at work. **"Oh yeah,"** Chrissie confessed a little while later, **"the record company probably did hype it. I quite genuinely don't know anything about how they run these business practices, but it does seem likely they could have operated like that.**

"Yet that doesn't explain why the album did as well as it did throughout the rest of the world," she now argues. **"It sold over a million copies in America. It went double platinum in Australia. And in Japan and across Europe it sold in truly vast quantities."**

"SO WHAT *EXACTLY* DON'T YOU LIKE ABOUT MY BOOTS?" PETE IN A LIGHTER MOMENT.

Although WEA refused to accept the allegations, not long afterwards managing director John Fruin was to lose his job. Furthermore, although he's remained reasonably unspecific in his remarks, Fruin *has* recently accepted that some irregularities did occur during the time WEA were 'marketing' The Pretenders' first LP.

"Certainly we put a lot behind them," says the former MD. **"We worked like mad to push them up the charts. Yet after a time we were able to stop work on them – they maintained their own momentum. But every act we had at the time was accused of being hyped. I will say though, that they became much bigger, much quicker than I had any right to expect, and that did surprise me. But having seen that here, I wasn't all that surprised about what happened for them in America."**

Dave Hill didn't know whether to be surprised or not. **"To be honest I think I put most of it down to good luck really,"** he attests. **"We hadn't put anything out in America until then, so there was a big impetus to buy the single ('Brass In Pocket' – the band's first US hit) and the album as soon as it came out. They'd heard all this stuff filtering through from Britain about the band. The singles were out on import – a whole buzz had been building. And when the radio picked up on the album and single, it just snow-balled.**

"There was no grand strategy, you know. In Britain, we did always plan to put out singles before an album. We could have put out an album (of sorts) straight after 'Sobbing', but it would have been wrong – that *was* a definite plan!

"But in America it really does seem to have been just down to luck. If it had been ready, we would have put out the album before Christmas. But instead, it was lucky that it wasn't ready to come out until January – it didn't get lost among all the other albums that came out before Christmas. Everyone claimed that in England the records were hyped to death. They *were* hyped, but you couldn't hype a number one single. Nor could you hype the fact that the LP came out on the same day the single got to number one. That was sheer coincidence."

With an American tour pending, The Pretenders arrived Stateside to the biggest reception of their career so far. A short visit turned into a five-month trek, as the group further developed their talents as a live act, consistently attracting hordes of new fans as they headed across country. By the time they arrived in New York at the end of the tour, the whole of America was aching for more. As for the band, they were just aching.

"They were definitely feeling the pressure by now," admits Hill.

"Everything had happened at once. The album zoomed up the US charts and we were off on tour – suddenly the next big thing. Chrissie didn't have a stable relationship, none of the guys did . . . it was a typical period of finding yourself. Maybe we shouldn't have toured so much, but what can you do? When you've got a runaway success, you've got to capitalise on it!"

The US tour had, in fact, been split into two legs, in the middle of which The Pretenders flew half way round the world, twice, in order to appear at a handful of European cities during the summer of 1980. They even tried to shoehorn a quick recording session into the schedule, but after three weeks (in Wessex studios) and only one resulting number ('I Go To Sleep') such plans had to be aborted through lack of interest. The success of their springtime UK single did interest them however. 'Talk Of The Town' made it to number eight.

By the time the conquering heroes returned to Blighty, it was clear to everyone that, although the tour had done wonders for their bank accounts, it had done nothing for their health. And they still had to endure a short series of home-based dates on top!

Even though the UK audiences were pleased to see them after so long an absence, the bartenders seemed less than impressed. Plagued from the outset, it was never going to be a good omen that the band would only be booked into hotels offering all-night drinking facilities.

Predictably then, with the British dates degenerating into one long party – punctuated only by the occasional bar brawl – the band's health grew steadily worse, particularly that of Honeyman-Scott who, by this time, had become the subject of serious concern.

Advised to refrain from the drink and drug abuse which was wrecking his body, Jimmy shrugged off such concerns and instead allowed journalists' attention to focus on the problems Chrissie was having with material for the second album.

CHRISSIE EATS MIKE, WHILE JIM LOOKS IMPRESSED.

GREAT PRETENDERS: PLAYING THE PROMOTIONAL GAME.

Although she'd actually co-written the 'Brass' single with the band's guitarist, this was an unusual practice, insomuch as sole responsibility for their material normally fell at Chrissie's feet. And whereas up till now she'd always had plenty of time to put together new songs, in whatever fashion that took her fancy, suddenly she was under pressure to produce hit records conveyor-belt style.

The minute their tour came to an end, The Pretenders were booked into the Pathé Marconi Studios in Paris with a view to recording album number two. Though the location may have been chosen in deference to Chrissie's love of the city, a more cynical motive lay at the heart of their decision. The British contingent within the group were now trying to become tax exiles!

"The very idea that there should be talk of such things rather sums up what people were expecting of the follow-up album," adjudicates Chris Thomas. **"It was the complete reverse of the first, where everything had been so relaxed and enjoyable. Chrissie had always been prepared to say, 'No!' during the making of the first LP, if she felt she was being pushed in the wrong direction. But now she felt hemmed in, and agreed to everything. And then those agreements became grudges.**

"Basically Chrissie was very aware of all this enormous pressure on her. She felt a tremendous sense of claustrophobia. It was a real strain for her. In fact, she didn't want to do the record at all. She'd become incredibly morose, regretting everything in which she'd become involved. She felt she wasn't doing it for her own reasons, the ones she'd started out making music for. She found all that pressure to come up with the goods very hard to take."

In order for the tax plan to work, the album had to be finished by Christmas, thus enabling the group to launch off on another world tour by the New Year. Needless to say, the album wasn't finished, the tour plans were postponed, and 'accountancy' became a rude word around The Pretenders camp. A real 10-quid-in-the-swear-box job. As for the flashy Paris studio – the band simply ran out of their allotted time.

In expectation of being finished with their record by the end of the year however, producer Chris Thomas had agreed to work with Elton John during the winter months. Consequently The Pretenders would be forced to take a break until spring 1981. But then, no one was going to complain about that too much.

As far as the British public were concerned, The Pretenders re-emerged in February, with a new single entitled 'Message Of Love'. In actual fact though, the group didn't get back to serious work until they returned to the studio some weeks later.

In the meantime the band were persuaded, for promotional reasons, to put out a 12-inch EP in America, featuring their recent UK single releases – as yet unavailable there. It was their first major mistake.

"The trouble was," explains Chrissie, **"everyone in England knew what an EP was, but they'd never had them in America. So when it came out, everyone thought it was an *album*, and people actually bought it as such. So it went into the American LP charts! And so we felt really hard-pressed not to put all of those songs ('Talk Of The Town', 'Message Of Love' and their respective B-sides) on the album. All the same, we wanted 'Message Of Love' on the album, 'cos that's what we'd recorded it for. Essentially it was a cock-up. A big cock-up."**

The EP held up the release of 'Pretenders II' still further, since now a time lapse had to be created in respect of the American market. When the album did finally appear, in August 1981, it came 20 months after the arrival of their first LP.

If The Pretenders had worried that the time element might destroy their momentum, and that the press would treat them harshly as a result, their concern was needless. The scheduling didn't seem to concern critics in the least – it was the songs they didn't like.

Honeyman-Scott took the reviews to heart, but Chrissie seemed to expect them, particularly in the light of her well-publicised private life, which seemed to be attracting more media interest than the record. Her recent affair with childhood idol and chief Kink Ray Davies (a married man at this time) was, according to some, directly responsible for destroying her sense of creativity. Apparently there was now 'too great a gulf between the subject matter of her

songs and the kind of life she chose to live' . . . which is funny really when the opening track on the album was titled 'The Adultress'.

"It was strange how it happened," reveals Ray. **"She just telephoned me in America one day, and . . . I mean, I don't meet people in the business at all, I'm rather an isolated character . . . but I *did* meet Chrissie, and we *did* fall in love. It was as simple as that, and nothing to do with work. We found we had so much common ground, quite apart from music."**

By the time The Pretenders were ready to go back on the road, Chrissie wasn't the only member of the band to have found romance. In fact, in April Jimmy had married a Texan model called Peggy-Sue Fender (how many guitarists could resist a surname like that!), while a month later, drummer Martin Chambers had wed Tracey Atkinson, a one-time secretary for the band's American company, Sire Records. The only member of the band without a shoulder to lean on was Pete Farndon, and pretty soon it began to show, with the bassist distancing himself more and more from the others.

"Well, I suppose, for a long time there'd been . . . because, you know, when Pete and I first started the band we got very close," Chrissie struggles to explain. **"I mean boyfriend and girlfriend type of close. And then we *stopped* going out with each other. Well, in that situation you usually don't want to see the person any more, or you really don't want to work with them. But we had to carry on and work together, and that was right back at the beginning of the band. So there was always this thing that wasn't quite right, y'know? Not really a rift, but a little bit of damage had been done, like a fissure had begun at an early stage.**

JIM'S WEDDING DAY, AND ANOTHER *MELODY MAKER* JOKE DOES THE ROUNDS.

THE PRESSURE ON: JIM AND CHRISSIE PROP EACH OTHER UP.

"Really," she confides, at last getting to grips with the nitty-gritty. **"The best way of summing up the whole situation, I can say it in one word . . . was heroin. And there's not really a lot you can say about heroin – end of story really. As Pete got more and more into his drug habit, his playing suffered for it. There was always this tradition of musicians who could be pretty well stoned, but could still get it together on-stage to play. Now Pete wasn't like that, his playing suffered for it. He got sloppy and he drank a lot, and he would drink whiskey so he was really a mess, and his playing got sloppier and sloppier."**

Problems aside, the fortnight prior to the release of the second album saw The Pretenders touring Britain for the second time in 10 months. After that, it was back to the States, and what would have been a gruelling 13-week tour, if it hadn't been for Chambers' argument with that light bulb.

But eight weeks in America *had* been enough to establish two significant facts. Firstly that whatever the critics wished to imply, The Pretenders were unquestionably one of the world's leading musical attractions. If they weren't, then the likes of Nils Lofgren and Bruce Springsteen wouldn't have been so keen to be seen jamming on-stage with them. The second, and sadder issue to impart, was that Farndon's days as a member of the group were fast becoming numbered.

The bass-player's concentration had slipped still further, and the guitarist had had enough. **"I can't tell you how much it infuriated Jim,"** Chrissie, a-hem, tells us. **"But it wasn't just Jim . . . we'd been on this tour, and we were all getting on each other's nerves, there's no doubt about it. Everyone was on their nerve endings. I mean, Martin punched that fuckin' lamp at one point, and so we even had to cancel the rest of the trip! And that's Martin, you see, this is the interesting point – Martin was always the buffer in the band.**

"We'd come off-stage and there'd be a horrible fight, and Jim would say, 'That was crap!' And Pete would throw the whole wardrobe over or whatever and I'd be getting uptight, just making matters worse, and then they might attack Martin. They'd say, 'You were playing fucking shit! You ruined the last song, your tempos were all over the place and you were complete crap!' And Martin would sit there and nod calmly and say, 'Yeah, I see your point, uh-huh, that's true.' You know what I mean? He was always the buffer for any situation, always the *fair* one. Now *he's* the one who punched a fucking lamp . . . so it even took its toll on Martin.

"Anyway, Jim wasn't getting on at all in this musical situation with Pete. And he took me aside on many occasions and said, you know, 'I'm not working with him again', and I didn't blame him.

"Pete had been taking smack for a long, long time, and his behaviour was completely erratic, as a junkie's is. One minute he'd be bubbling over, he'd be over-zealous in his enthusiasm for something 'cos he'd just gotten high. Next thing we'd be steaming away on something and then, 15 minutes later, he's completely nodded out or something. It was infuriating. Jimmy couldn't stand it.

"YOU'D BE STROPPY IF *YOUR* HAIR WAS ALWAYS IN YOUR EYES." CHRISSIE'S GLUM LOOK.

"It was clear that Pete's situation wasn't getting any better, and musically things just weren't happening either. Actually, that's when I stopped reading our reviews because the journalists were all talking about how it was becoming like a heavy metal backing group. Pete was getting very heavy-handed in his playing, while Jimmy and I were pulling more and more towards this lyrical/melodic thing – it was making us go too extreme to balance out.

"Pete was also completely lost in this whole rock-star pose thing. He was one of those unfortunate people who saw the picture of himself in the paper and thought that was him. He forgot it was just a photograph of a guy. He thought it was *him*, with the quiff and the kamikaze pilot suit and that wasted look. And that was it. We just couldn't carry on. Martin was adamant he couldn't take it any more. He didn't want to watch the guy shooting up in hotel rooms any more."

Amid public rumours that the bassist was now a registered drug addict, the other three decided to put up with him for the time being and consequently made plans to return to the States in the New Year, with a view to playing those previously postponed shows. In the meantime, they kept themselves active with a short burst of UK concerts in the run-up to Christmas 1981. Due to kick-off in Dublin however, the tour almost ended before it had begun, with the accident-prone drummer again coming a cropper!

"Before we'd even done the soundcheck for that first date," recounted Jimmy in a desperate effort to keep a straight face, "we were all in my hotel room attending one of my discos – a Vera Lynn disco that day, 'Stars On 45' of Vera Lynn. Martin came down and he was juggling with these Guinness bottles, and – *whoops!* – the other hand went!"

"We fell apart, actually," says Martin, taking up the story, "because it was just so funny. Though I don't think our manager saw it that way. He went a funny kind of pale greeny-yellow. There were extreme spouts of blood. I just rammed a finger over it, bunged it under the tap and went off to hospital. They injected it about a dozen times, put some stitches in, and then I ran to the soundcheck. No matter what, I was going to have carried on. If my finger had been severed completely, I would still have carried on."

Banned from any further acts of death-defying stupidity, Chambers made it through the tour OK, and the group were able to make up that month in America after all. After which, a quick trip round Japan, Australia, and Hong Kong would finally fulfil their globe-trotting commitments for some considerable time.

It was now April 1982, and they were all knackered. So the boys in the band decided to have a quick break wherever they ended up. As luck would have it, they'd ended up in Bangkok.

Not entirely rested then, they eventually went their separate ways, although Jimmy and Pete both flew back to Tokyo, where the former would meet up with his wife (working there on a modelling assignment), and the latter would get married to a girl he'd known for a full two weeks! The duo would never work together again.

On Saturday June 12, Jimmy returned to Britain, and was promptly called to a Sunday meeting at Dave Hill's London office. Chrissie and Martin were also present during this, the final stage of discussions surrounding the future of Pete Farndon. Labelled reckless and irresponsible, the bass-player was deemed to be a dramatically altered personality and, as such, no longer fitted into the framework of the band. The following afternoon, Farndon was sacked. Hill did the deed himself, and cited 'differences of musical opinion' as the final straw. Rumour has it that 'slugging Ray Davies backstage one night' might have provided sounder reasoning.

Either way, with the bassist gone, and a studio booked for two weeks' time (they were scheduled to record the next single, 'Back On The Chain Gang'), responsibility suddenly fell on the guitarist to fill in on bass, until such time as alternative arrangements might be made. This wouldn't present any real problem, Hill was busily explaining to the press on Wednesday June 16, because Jimmy was an especially accomplished musician. What the manager didn't know at this time however, was that Honeyman-Scott was lying dead in a London flat.

On Tuesday June 15, the day after Farndon's sacking, Jimmy attended a charity show given by Clare Grogan's Altered Images at The Venue, just opposite Victoria Station. His drinking was described as 'moderate' but he *had* apparently scored some cocaine from a London dealer earlier that evening. Indeed the autopsy report did find traces of cocaine in his system, and also suggested that other unspecified substances had been located in his stomach. Add to this the rumour that he is supposed to have snorted a line of heroin before going to sleep that night in a friend's flat, and one's left wondering why – if this was his regular lifestyle – the guitarist hadn't passed away months ago.

"In a sick kind of way, I'm sure that Jimmy would've said he wanted to die the way he did," remarks former live-in lover Sharon Chevin, who'd been among his party of friends that fatal night. **"In fact, he probably would've been quite proud of himself, though obviously to have lived a few more years wouldn't have hurt. I do think he was on something of a self-destruction number, and was trying to push into his life as much as he could. Also, perhaps he didn't realise he was as ill as he was. He always wanted more than he had. He was after**

> " THE FIRST THING I NOTICED WAS THAT HE WAS IN HIS SLEEPING POSITION, WITH THE BACK OF HIS WRISTS ON HIS FOREHEAD . . . I KNEW HE HAD DIED IN HIS SLEEP. "

something that he thought he desperately needed, though in the end he didn't really know what it was he wanted. He was searching for love and happiness and contentment, and I think he tried so hard to get it that he blew it."

Fellow band member Martin Chambers had his own ideas about Jimmy's death however. **"The problem was,"** the drummer tried to explain shortly afterwards, **"Jimmy didn't have any real upbringing at all. It was a similar situation with Pete, though his mum's great. But they both came from broken homes, and both had similar attitudes. They would hardly ever think about the next few days, let alone about the future. I *do* think about the future, and about what I'd like to be doing, and I don't think there's anything wrong with thinking about what I might be doing in 10 years' time.**

"It's not as simple as either of them being destroyed by wanton self-destruction. It's a question really of not seeing too well past the end of your nose. I can't understand that. Everything to me is very, very simple. That is basically the idea, keeping it like that.

"But as soon as you get in a band, that gets difficult enough. And when you get in a *successful* band, everything becomes the complete opposite of simple. Life suddenly becomes very complicated, with all sorts of pressures and responsibilities. It's one of those situations where you really have to keep your eyes set straight ahead, and not be distressed by all this rubbish that goes along with it."

Along with manager Hill, Chambers was one of the first on the scene when the guitarist's body was found. **"The first thing I noticed was that Jimmy was in his sleeping position, with the back of his wrists on his forehead,"** the drummer sadly recalls. **"So at least, in a way, I knew he had died in his sleep. He hadn't died violently. There was a policeman there, and he kept asking me questions, but I just couldn't turn my back on Jimmy. And when the copper finally got my attention, he asked me for my autograph. Funnily enough, I gave it to him."**

Jimmy was buried in Hereford a week after his death. No Pretenders' music was played after the service but, instead, Peggy-Sue invited mourners to listen to a compilation of the star's favourite Beach Boys songs. The tape began, as indeed it ended, with what she thought would have been Jimmy's own choice – 'Darlin'. And with that, the man that Chris Spedding always referred to as 'the *sound* of The Pretenders' was gone. He was 25.

The obituaries came flooding in of course, most of them telling the same story – one which Chrissie had always known, but would only later endorse.

"Jim was a tremendously talented guy. He was great at adding those neat little hook lines – I never added any *lyrical* hooklines – he

did them, usually with melodic guitar. You could say it was the very essence of our sound . . . How could he not be missed?"

With the bassist sacked and the guitarist dead, few believed The Pretenders would, even *could* rise from the ashes. The music press predicted it was the end of the road, and it may well have been had The Pretenders not been required to produce three albums under the terms of their recording contract.

If Chrissie was going to keep it going she had to move fast. As it later transpired, the driving-force of The Pretenders was three-months pregnant at the time of Jimmy's death. If a new single wasn't recorded soon, who knows when they'd have got around to it? Probably never. Which, as Chrissie is keen to emphasise, would have been a further waste.

"You work so hard for two years to get into a position where you're allowed to make records, and get paid to do it. And a lot of people really blow it. You've simply got to keep the thing ticking over . . . finish what you've started. I'm not particularly proud of it, or even think it's that exciting. It's certainly not important either – it's just what I'm finishing off."

'Back On The Chain Gang' was to have been the next vinyl commitment, so Chrissie stuck with it. Hiring temporary assistance from Nick Lowe's Rockpile sidekick, guitarist Billy Bremner, and Big Country's well-respected Tony Butler (bass), she and Martin Chambers went back into the studio. Thankfully Chris Thomas was available to lend a helping hand.

"Chris Thomas, in my estimation, bailed us out and saved our asses on that one," claims Chrissie. "We had a Pretenders sound alright, which had been developed by the four of us – me and Pete, Jimmy and Martin – over a year before the first album, but it was

SUFFERING FOR THEIR ART: CHRISSIE'S TROUSERS GIVE HER HELL.

Chris who helped us develop it in the studio. We always maintained he was a fifth member of the band. With someone like that you just can't pinpoint a specific contribution, he'd just done so many extra things – a little bit of keyboards here and there with Jim, a little guitar arpeggio on something, a little sound effect. On 'Bad Boys Get Spanked' he tapped a bottle of Evian water throughout the whole song – you can hear it at the end of the track. I walked in there one day and he was hitting a motorcycle helmet with a piece of wood!

"So anyway, at this very difficult moment in our so-called career, with Chris's help, Martin and I could preserve something of what we had built over the years. Without Chris, Martin and I might have lost our way altogether. Maybe we *could* have carried on, made a record. But I would have been in two minds about using the name, The Pretenders."

'Back On The Chain Gang' was finally unleashed on October 2, 1982, and despite the fact that *Melody Maker* didn't like it very much, the song sailed up the charts, eventually anchoring at number seven. This was The Pretenders' first single for a year ('I Go To Sleep' had preceded it the previous November), and the first to reach the Top 10 in the American charts. It would also be their last for another 12 months.

In the meantime Chrissie would withdraw from public life, busy herself with professional commitments (getting a new band together), give birth to a bouncing baby girl (Natalie), contemplate marriage to the father (Ray Davies), and battle to overcome the shock of yet another tragic event – the death of Pete Farndon.

After his unceremonious departure from the band Farndon had, ironic as it may sound, talked of setting up a new group with another of Chrissie's ex-lovers, Nick Kent. At the time of his death though, the bass-player had been rehearsing at Hammersmith studios with original Police guitarist Henri Padovani, former Clash drummer Topper Heddon, one-time Blockheads keyboard-player Mickey Gallagher, and Hot Club singer Steve Allen. They were all set, or so it is said, to sign a recording deal.

Farndon's body was found by his wife, Conover-Lee, on April 14, 1983. Slumped in the bath of the couple's Kensington home, a nearby syringe told the ugly tale. While Farndon almost certainly died of drowning, the inquest was obliged to record a verdict of drug addiction. Heroin and cocaine were the culprits and *he*, fact fans will be keen to learn, was just 30.

"The guy blew it," Chrissie says. "He shot up a speed ball and drowned in the bath. It's not really my idea of a beautiful rock 'n' roll image – the tattooed arm, hanging out of the tub, turning blue, with a syringe stuck in it but that's what it came to in the end."

CHAPTER FOUR

Crawling From The Wreckage

CHRISSIE WITH, L-R, CHAMBERS, FARNDON AND HONEYMAN-SCOTT. A HARD ACT TO FOLLOW.

It would be cruel to infer that Chrissie Hynde hadn't been deeply hit by such a tragic run of events. She wasn't quick to make any 'I'm terribly upset' speeches, but most of us can understand that.

"I just didn't want to talk to the press," she says, offering an explanation to the few who feel they need one. **"I didn't wanna flippantly write any epitaphs in a few lines, which is what it always looks like, y'know? 'He wuz a great guy!' said Paul McCartney after they stood outside his house for three days waiting, kind of thing. What can you say when someone's obviously been an integral part of your life, and has really touched your life, and when they die it's like a part of you has died as well?**

"Let's make no mistake here, it was a hell of a fucking shock when Pete died, but it wasn't *surprising*. Because it never is when you know

that someone's so far into it. You always know the phone might ring, and that you'll get the news. Every day you live with that possibility. In fact, when I heard the news about Pete, I only needed to be told his name to know what had happened. The manager phoned me up and said, 'Farndon', and that was it. I said, 'I'll talk to you later', and hung up. He didn't have to say anything else. I just had to hear that one word, and I knew what he meant by it. After that, whenever he called me up I was afraid to speak to him . . .

"But Jim, that was out of the blue. Out of the blue and into the black I'm afraid, for Mr Scott. Jimmy *was* a terrible drug abuser, a drug *fiend*. When I met him he was a speed freak, and his guts were so rotten on the inside, he'd abused his health so badly . . .

"Let's face it, these weren't two of the healthiest guys you've ever met that we're talking about here. But it was so abrupt with Jim . . . and y'know, Pete turned around and it was like, 'So you throw *me* out and *he's* the one that kills himself on drugs.' And poor Pete never understood, he just never understood. That's my big regret, I never sat down and talked to him about it, we never did make it up. But that's what happens when someone dies. There's always gonna be these regrets."

Would her major regret be that neither she, nor anyone else connected with the band, had been able to do anything to stop the rot? Couldn't someone have saved Jimmy and Pete from themselves?

"Well that's very tricky," says Chrissie, "Because you can really resent that . . . I don't want to make a big deal out of this indulgence, although it would be unrealistic of me to say it was no big deal – I mean two of my guys are dead now because of it, so you have to face the music. The *best* thing in that situation, if you could see that someone like Jimmy couldn't say no (to the suppliers hanging round backstage), would be to try and weed out the assholes and not let people like that around us. As soon as someone came round you could say, 'Hey Jim, that guy's an asshole!' But it's too late then."

Happily, Chrissie was able to save herself *before* it became too late. Although her involvement with drugs could never be compared with the desperate dependency of a Scott or a Farndon, the fact remains that the nervous performer did like her drink – and was often seen swigging vodka out of a bottle long after the rest of the band had quit the post-gig ligs.

"I was never what you'd call a social drinker," she quips, "much more an antisocial one. I wasn't so much one of the boys when I got into a bar and got drunk. A drunken woman's different to a drunken man. I was becoming like the kid whose mom was an embarrassing

> THE MANAGER PHONED ME UP AND SAID, 'FARNDON', AND THAT WAS IT . . . I JUST HAD TO HEAR THAT ONE WORD, AND I KNEW WHAT HE MEANT BY IT.

alcoholic, I was becoming that woman. I didn't get jolly, I started a fight."

Indeed, for all the disreputable activities of her colleagues, it was Chrissie who made the headlines when, one night in Memphis, the drunken singer got into a fight and was subsequently taken for a ride in a local patrol car. Chrissie kicked shit out of the car alright but came a cropper when its contents – a couple of equally boisterous boys in blue – took vengeance by shoving her in the slammer till morning.

"The band hated my guts for that, and it *was* pretty awful. The funny thing about it though was that it gave us a lot of good old rock 'n' roll publicity, the kind that some bands thrive on to make them more interesting."

Strangely in some respects, as Pete and Jimmy's indulgence had increased, so Chrissie's had waned. This may be due partly to an ever-increasing confidence in herself as a public figure but, most likely, she just decided to get her act together – and succeeded.

"It would have been around the time I met Ray (Davies), I suppose," Chrissie reflects. **"I just woke up one day and thought, if I don't really clean up my act . . . I realised there wasn't going to be much of a future. Ray wasn't going to stay around, and I couldn't see why anyone would *want* to hang around with me much longer, the state I was in.**

"Obviously everyone has their own story about how they came to a crisis point, but . . . I remember Johnny Thunders came up to me with a great big purple lip. I don't know where *he'd* fallen down, but he was actually coming up to me and saying, 'Wow, Chrissie, you gotta get it together, you gotta clean up yer act.' And I knew I was in bad shape, y'know? 'Cause he'd seen me the night before and I was in worse shape than *he* was!

"But that's not to say I want to play on anything that's happened to me. I haven't had it harder than, I dunno, Lorraine in Croydon, my life isn't any harder or more exceptional than anyone else that I can see. I don't want to create this false rock 'n' roll mystique, that I'm the 'survivor', that I've had it bad. I don't like mentioning names, but I don't want to be Marianne Faithfull, always talking about that sort of thing. You pay your money and you take your choice, *bub*! If you wanna OD and die or become a lush under Charing Cross bridge or whatever – go ahead.

"And, you know, it really *isn't* like any mystery or anything. People say to me, how did I escape? Well I didn't shoot smack for one thing! Sure there were always creeps hanging around the dressing

room with their little packets of cocaine as a calling card to get in. But to me there was always an exit somewhere. I'd put my sweatshirt and jeans on and walk out through the audience that were hanging around, say excuse me and sneak back to my hotel room. If I did stick around, I'd see all these chicks hanging out backstage looking like what they thought I was supposed to look like. I had someone ask me if I was one of the roadcrew once, ha-ha! So yeah, I'd just keep a low profile and get the hell outa there!"

RAY DAVIES: HERO, FRIEND AND LOVER . . . FINALLY DITCHED.

One of the great ironies of this particular stage in The Pretenders story is that, before the break-up of the original line-up – and the subsequent deaths of two of its members – plans had been afoot to augment the group with an additional guitarist anyway. As prime instigator of the move Jimmy, who had also been a credible keyboard player, saw tremendous possibilities for developing the band's sound, if only a suitable candidate could be located.

As fate would have it, the night before he died, Jimmy found his man – Robbie McIntosh, a fairly anonymous muso who'd previously played with a fairly anonymous group called Night. In the space of 24 hours then, this new name had gone from 'possible sidekick' to 'probable replacement', although the final decision would now rest with Chrissie.

Even before the birth of her daughter, Ms Hynde (she never did marry the famous Kink) determined to sort out a new working line-up for the group. And though she'd been aware of Jimmy's recommendation, Chrissie nonetheless chose to go through the process of advertising for, and auditioning realistic candidates, a procedure she later regretted.

"We were inundated with applications," she recalls, sounding curiously surprised. **"I got tons of tapes, photographs of guys in rock 'n' roll poses . . .**

"But then Robbie walked in, and there was little doubt that he'd be the right choice, like, straight away. And it was such a relief, 'cos we still had hundreds waiting to audition. But we knew there was no point, unless we were going to video the remaining auditions and put it out as some kinda comedy film. What a scream – we had our Johnny Thunders clones, our Johnny Thunders-cum-Keith Richards clones, they were all there. I know Robbie felt kinda embarrassed about applying, but we were sure pleased he did – even if he was a guitar bore, ha-ha! All he could do was play guitar and listen to old records. He was just like Jimmy Scott in that way!"

In much the same way as the Hereford trio had come as a package during the late seventies, so Robbie McIntosh now came with *his* own bass player, Malcolm Foster. They'd previously worked together in a pub band called Dean Martin's Dog, so that was that. How could Chrissie refuse them? **"Instant band!"** Chrissie exclaims. **"Sounds easy, doesn't it? But in fact we were damn lucky the group got together so quickly."**

Rehearsing by December 1982 then, the new line-up started work on the third album fairly pronto, only breaking for the birth of Chrissie's baby in January. Whether or not such emotions had been heightened by her condition, it's difficult to say, but Chrissie *did* find it harder getting used to her new working colleagues than she would ever readily admit.

"I went through periods of feeling almost a sort of resentment

toward the others in a very irrational, emotional sort of way," she explains. **"The first time I saw one of them – I think it was Malcolm – walk in with a Pretenders T-shirt on, I thought, 'Who is *he* to be wearing a Pretenders shirt?' It's like if your wife died, and you had a new girlfriend who you really loved. But one day she went through your wife's wardrobe and walked in wearing her clothes. No matter how you felt about this woman, your reaction would be, 'Hang on! That's not cool'."**

Although isolated in the main, such self-indulgences did still occur, even after some months of working together.

"While overall we enjoyed making that third album, there were certainly moments when it wasn't a barrel of monkeys," Chrissie admits. **"One day someone brought in the previous album, just to compare sounds of something we were working on. I hadn't listened to any of that stuff since we'd last played it. While it was on, I found it very difficult to look at the other guys. I had to leave the room. "'Chain Gang' and 'Ohio' were the songs that Jimmy and I had been working on before all those things happened. We used to run through them during soundchecks, and had planned on recording them. Sometimes they sounded great. It was obviously frustrating, not to mention an emotional experience, to do these songs now."**

PERIOD LINE-UP: L-R, CHAMBERS, McINTOSH, HYNDE AND FOSTER.

SENSE OF RELIEF: CHRISSIE AND ROBBIE SEEM SATISFIED WITH THEIR LOT.

If getting the new group together had been an emotional strain, taking it on the road could only be worse. Chrissie was terrified, not so much because of the critics, but more because of her decision to take her new-born baby with her as well.

"I'll tell ya how I felt about it," she said. **"I felt more apprehensive than ever, not just because it was a new band and everything, but mainly because of what it was doing to my private life. Yes, apprehensive is the word. I felt apprehensive because I was gonna be taking this baby with me, and I was worried about her, although I felt sure that she'd be alright. I just wouldn't have gone on tour if I thought it wouldn't be alright for her. But she was young enough that as long as she got what she needed, I knew she'd be happy. I didn't know if I was gonna be able to take her in a couple of years. I didn't want her first words to be 'room service'."**

In the event, Chrissie soon became more worried about the performing potential of the new group than she did of her reputation as a mother, and so, putting the studio work on ice, decided to take the opportunity of rehearsing The Pretenders in front of a live audience early that summer. Not for them the quiet backwaters of a Wakefield club, this line-up would play *its* first ever show supporting David Bowie at California's prestigious US Festival 1983. New band and new baby, both coped admirably.

Heralded a resounding success, the performance paved the way for a string of US dates, followed by a fast plane to London, permitting the band a speedy return to recording commitments.

In touch with tradition, Hynde again employed Chris Thomas at the controls, only this time invited one or two 'guesting' musicians to appear on the sessions as well. Amongst others, Andrew Bodnar (bass) and Paul Carrack (keyboards) were spotted trotting into Air Studios to augment The Pretenders line-up – only to trot out again, a few quid richer.

The first product from this period to reach the public's attention was the Christmas single, '2000 Miles', which eventually saw light of day on November 26. It was the *NME*'s turn to pour scorn this time, reckoning the record didn't stand a snowflake's chance in hell of being a success – a curious claim considering the time of year. In fact, the song did OK, spending 9 weeks on the chart, peaking at number 15, while somewhat heroically serving to welcome the new album, 'Learning To Crawl'. It was their first to be granted a title.

> HAVING A BABY IS A VERY NATURAL THING TO HAPPEN. IT GIVES YOU OTHER THINGS TO THINK ABOUT . . .

"Well, the one thing we didn't do on our first two albums was title them," Chrissie explains. **"I find that the hard part. The first one you can get away with, you can just call it after yourselves and here we are. On the second one we really copped out, 'Pretenders II', but maybe it wasn't that interesting to warrant a title, I don't know. But we really couldn't go with 'Pretenders III'.**

"'Learning To Crawl' was, in the obvious way, influenced by the fact that I had a baby now – who incidentally *had* just learned to crawl. But on a more profound level, I suppose, the band had pretty much had to rebuild itself from scratch.

"But there were other reasons for that title. 'Learning To Crawl', for me . . . oh, God, I prayed I would never have to explain this to anyone, it was simply the way that I felt, at that point in my life."

At that point in her life, Chrissie was learning a lot of things. Not least, she'd learned to come to terms with herself and her own dominating nature. Always the brash and outspoken leader, she'd simultaneously tried to quash the role by constantly claiming herself to be 'just another member of the band.' This was clearly never the case, for Chrissie had not only clinched the record deal on her own, she'd then written almost all the songs, given nearly all the interviews and been highlighted by just about every spotlight that had ever been flickered in The Pretenders' direction. Damn it, she even wore a T-shirt with '*My Way Or The Highway*' printed across her chest!

But now, in her 32nd year, Chrissie began to look on the burden of leadership with new eyes.

"Well yeah, I suppose I always tried to shoulder some of that attention in the early days . . . Before, I'd always at least attempt to have someone else involved whenever the press came knocking on our door. And I'd only have photos done of the band, I would never have dreamed of doing a front cover, of anything, where it was just me – except you get some sneaky little bastard who will crop the picture, who'll agree to use the whole group on the cover, and the next thing you know they've cropped out the group. I wouldn't even

be photographed without the rest of the band, just in case. But what a pair of scissors and a diseased mind can do, y'know?

"But now, it was a bit unrealistic to think that it was this group, The Pretenders, like a young pop group, 'cos we all knew what'd happened, and we were older now, and at that point I had to take some responsibility for my role in the band. I was the sort of spokesperson I suppose, and I was just owning up a little bit, maybe. Things had changed."

'Learning To Crawl' first appeared in the shops during January 1984, its release coinciding neatly with the line-up's début tour of the UK. A trip which would prove a very different one for the band's leader this time round.

"Instead of making a drunken idiot of myself every night, I had to go back to my room," Chrissie laughs. "Having a baby is a very natural thing to happen. It gives you other things to think about, but then at the age of 32 you're not just thinking about sex and drugs and rock 'n' roll. You go beyond the things that you might have been talking about when you were 25.

"It must have crossed the minds of all the Mick Jaggers and so on, am I too old? They all said they wouldn't be doing it when they turned 30, because they all started when they were 18. Are we supposed to still be thinking about getting laid and getting stoned? 'They said we're too young to be in love.' It's kinda hard when you're talking to someone who's 42-years-old!

"I don't think of rock as youth culture music anyway. To me it's contemporary music. Mind you, a lot of the stuff now is like music for 8-year-olds, real kiddie stuff. I can't relate to a lot of it. I'd never pander to an audience of 19-year-old boys. Thirty-year-old cocktail waitresses with a couple of kids, surely that's my audience. I don't really feel I have anything to say. I'm just trying to do my little thing, which is exactly the same as it always was. I'm doing what's relevant to me. There's a song on that album, 'Learning To Crawl', that's all about washing clothes in a laundromat. That's more relevant to me than sitting around counting scars on a junkie's arms. I don't see most of those guys any more, the ones that are left."

Chrissie wasn't seeing much of her live-in boyfriend by this stage either. At the end of the UK sprint, The Pretenders were off on a world tour, the singer seemingly content to leave domestic traumas behind her.

Chrissie and Ray had always shared a fairly volatile private life. Indeed, the Pretender once described it herself as, **"The most violent relationship I've ever seen or heard of. We once watched *Who's Afraid Of Virginia Woolf?* and laughed at how mild it all seemed."**

Nor had things been assisted any by friends and associates around them. It's generally believed that the rest of The Pretenders grew bored by Davies' ever-increasing presence, while Ray's own brother would later reciprocate with a lorry-load of ill-feeling at Chrissie's expense.

"It was immediately after Jimmy Scott's death," Chrissie says, recalling the occasion she'd flown to New York to be with Ray. **"As The Kinks were getting their standing ovation that particular night, Ray went to the microphone and said, 'I want you to say hello . . .' and he said something very flattering like, ' . . . to a really great singer,' or something. And he sort of dragged me out from the side of the stage, and everyone stood up and clapped. I knew it was really their way of saying sorry, the audience showing me some sympathy. When I walked off, I bumped into Dave (Davies), and he punched me and spat in my face and said never, ever to go near their stage again. Suffice to say I didn't. I'd really like to forget all about that though, because it's probably something between them, and I'd rather stay out of that sort of thing altogether."**

If that seemed like a low-point however, the current situation was even more disheartening. Davies hadn't wanted her to go on the road after 'Learning To Crawl' came out, and although she went anyway, Chrissie was forced to admit that professional aspirations were adding further fuel to their regular feuding.

"Ray wasn't very happy about it at all," Chrissie admits. **"Not because I was taking the baby on tour (Robbie McIntosh's wife and child would also be in attendance), but because I was going on tour at all. *He* went on tour as well but, same meat different gravy."**

The bottom line, of course, was that Chrissie followed her instincts, and shepherded The Pretenders around the globe during the first half of 1984. And although the band particularly enjoyed the launch of the tour in Britain, it'll no doubt be the Australian leg that their leader will look back on with the fondest memories. For it was there, on the other side of the world, that Chrissie was to meet up with Simple Minds, and their lead singer Jim Kerr.

"I'd never even *seen* Simple Minds before Australia," admits Chrissie. **"And it was fairly mind-blowing because I'd heard about this neo-psychedelic thing, which didn't really interest me because I was part of the real psychedelia in its time – the late sixties. It didn't seem like it would mean anything to see a psychedelic band if everyone wasn't tripping on LSD. But when I saw them, they *were* psychedelic. And, as it turns out, they *were* tripping on LSD, so that made perfect sense. I was shocked, they were so great!"**

Even though they were touring the Continent at the same time, the story of

CHRISSIE AND JIM KERR: WEDDED BLISS, ER, SORT OF.

Chrissie and Jim's attachment still seemed as strange as it was uncharacteristically romantic.

Seven years her junior, the Glaswegian singer had grown up with an almost completely different perception of the values and worth of contemporary music. But if their target audiences might have appeared poles apart, the nature of their individual personalities would prove more than enough to compensate. Over-compensate some might have said (Ray Davies for one?), for within just four months of having met, Chrissie and Jim were man and wife.

"They just went and did it," reports Dave Hill. **"There was nobody there from either of their bands. It was a private affair – Chrissie is a very private person."**

If it had been any more private it wouldn't have been legal. After breaking the news to Davies at the last minute, Chrissie met up with Jim at a New York registry office where, in the company of a minister and a pair of witnesses, they sped off in a horse-drawn carriage round Central Park. And that's where the vows were taken. Dedicated fashion followers take note – they both wore white.

With hectic schedules upon them, the happy loving couple weren't able to honeymoon in the manner in which they'd have liked – i.e together, so instead they burned a few royalty cheques through phoning each other every day.

But when autumn came around, by an extraordinary stroke of 'luck', The Pretenders and Simple Minds found themselves touring the States on the same bill. This of course made communication a lot more convenient, not to say a significantly more interesting experience . . . **"I want to congratulate Jim Kerr,"** Chrissie told a Long Island audience during yet another in a long line of sell-out shows. **"He's just found out his wife is pregnant."**

CHAPTER FIVE

Nappy Days Are Here Again

ROBBIE: FINDING THE GOING TOUGH.

"I'd never even picked up a baby before I had one. I just thought they were like a load of Martians who had nothing to do with me. But the morning I had my first child, Natalie, I got out of my bed and walked down the corridor to have a good look at her, and she was just this tiny, little helpless thing. And I looked at the other babies, and you start to see that they are individuals. they're all different – different behaviour, character and personality.

"I remember saying that I was going to feed her for one year, because I thought it would be good for her. People think it's weird because it's inconvenient. My God! . . . *inconvenient!!* . . . **some people really do have the weirdest sense of values."**

Chrissie Hynde wouldn't be a good person to talk to about planning a family – **"These people make me sick that say they're gonna plan a family** to fit in around their career" – and she certainly wouldn't entertain the notion that motherhood and rock 'n' roll don't mix – **"It would feel more odd to me if I *didn't* have kids!"** Nonetheless Chrissie does accept that, at this stage in our social history, it is no longer unusual for career-minded women to forgo the opportunity of having children.

"Maybe it's not *unusual*," she concedes, **"but it is unnatural, on a purely humanistic level . . . people get carried away with their own self-indulgence if they're having sex and they're not having children. It can only make you go slightly off the rails mentally, because it's just not natural. You shouldn't be fucking all the time and not getting pregnant – just 'cos you're taking drugs and stuff – because emotionally, everything else is going to get out of balance."**

Hubbie Jim chose to be present at the birth of *their* first child – Chrissie's second. Another girl, the bonnie lass weighed in at 7 lbs 10 oz. They named her Yasmin. And then Simple Minds went back to work.

In commercial terms, 1984 hadn't been the best possible year for The Pretenders. 'Learning To Crawl' only spent 16 weeks on the chart (their previous LPs had been around for 35 and 27 weeks respectively) and never did make it to the Top 10. Furthermore the singles, 'Middle Of The Road' and The Persuaders cover, 'Thin Line Between Love And Hate', had to be regarded as relative failures for a band thought to thrive on radio success. **"I never did understand the thing about 'Thin Line',"** Chrissie confesses. **"Everyone told me it was their favourite Pretenders single, yet no one bought it."** Only reaching 49 on the UK chart, it was probably their biggest disappointment since the 1981 flop, 'Day After Day', and critics could surely be forgiven for thinking the writing was on the wall.

It would have silenced many a cynic, had The Pretenders been able to bounce back and suddenly unleash a series of hit records the following year. But with Chrissie having just given birth to her second daughter, the band's leader did rather seem to have her hands full for the time being. Not only that but, all of a sudden, much of that hard-as-nails determination seemed to have been dispelled from her make-up. Was she losing the urge to carry on?

"Well, I suppose I must have mellowed slightly," she declares. **"At that stage, just the fact that I was still alive proves I must have mellowed, because people don't carry on that wild and get away with it too long. But I'd had a couple of kids, and that really slows you down, y'know. Being a mother is like a full-time occupation.**

"Any mother will tell you that you need a degree in physics to get two kids ready when it's raining outside, to get them to the shops when they're screaming at the top of their lungs, to get them out of the check-out counter when there's every sweet known to man at

CHRISSIE WITH ALI CAMPBELL.

their eye-level. It just occurred to me suddenly, that the mother is quite literally too often left holding the baby. Spare a thought for the single woman who's not going to do anything else but look after her child for 10 years."

All this isn't to say that Mrs Kerr was unhappy with her lot however – far from it. "I couldn't have been more delighted with my lot. I was doing what I wanted to do. I've always found it healthy to be around children. The problems that you have don't relate to their lives at all."

The main problem Chrissie was having at this time was motivating herself to get back to work again. And indeed, if it hadn't been for her husband, she may never have managed it.

Each day during the ensuing weeks, Jim would phone home from his latest port of call. "I've just gotten off the plane, have you written anything?" he'd ask. "Why should I write anything?" his wife would retort. "Because that's what you do! When you're filling in your passport and it says occupation, you put songwriter," Jim insisted. He was right, and she knew it.

For all her attempts at scribbling together some new songs for The Pretenders, it's odd to reflect that Chrissie's only record release in 1985 would turn out to be a rendition of a 20-year-old hit – which she then went and recorded with UB40. As to whose idea it was to cover Sonny and Cher's classic, well, that rather depends upon who you choose to believe. Chrissie doesn't have any doubts however.

"If you ever met any of UB40," she chuckles, **"you'd know those guys could *never* have had the idea to do 'I Got You Babe', though since it got to number one they swear blind they did. It was *my* idea.**

"I went to see them initially in 1980 at The Rock Garden, at Pete Farndon's recommendation, with the notion of inviting them to support us on our first British tour. They were so good I felt sheepish about asking them, but they agreed. Our paths crossed many times later and doing 'I Got You Babe' was frequently discussed, usually after we'd had several vats of wine and they'd put me in a taxi back to my hotel. I said to Ali Campbell, 'With my face and your voice we can't go wrong', and eventually he agreed.

"I remember going to UB40's studio, with the all-time unfortunate name of The Abattoir. We recorded the song completely live. Ali is a brilliant singer, a legend. I met Cher at *Live Aid* and told her I'd nicked her song, but she didn't understand what I meant. The word 'nicked' seemed to throw her completely. I forgot I'm an anglophile."

If it hadn't been for 'Sir' Bob's extraordinary charity bash, The Pretenders may not have set foot on the live stage that year. Performing at the Philadelphia end of proceedings, they went down pretty well, though not as well as Simple Minds, or as well as Chrissie's live duet with Ali Campbell!

Indeed it was *Live Aid*, or rather the preparation for the event, that led Chrissie to the conclusion that The Pretenders were in desperate need of fresh blood.

"The feeling struck me the day we decided to do a warm up for the event, in some small club," she recollects. **"At this little rehearsal someone suggested that we might even do a gig there, that very night – just do a set in the club. Well, we hadn't played for, like, six months or even longer. So we asked the band there if we could go on and do a set before them, and they were cool about it. Since we were in a club though, I said, 'Let's try a couple of things more like a club set' – we'd come from playing places like Madison Square Garden, y'know, that kinda size. There was one song called 'Soul Of The Man', the B-side of Fontella Bass's 'Rescue Me' single, a very bluesy thing.**

"Now, Robbie's like a real blues player. I always had to steer him away from playing blues on everything. He's the guy at a party who ends up at five in the morning looking through the album collection and pulling out all the old Chuck Berry records. If I left the studio for 10 minutes, just to go to the toilet or something, I'd come back and it was 'the blues', y'know? I'd go, 'I can't trust you for 10 minutes!'

"So . . . this day I said, 'How about let's do a blues song?' Because we're in a club right, so why not? So Robbie was wailing away, and at that moment, that day, I suddenly realised that the band just didn't have the *feel*. We couldn't transpose our thing from a great big arena to a club! I guess it happens to a lot of bands, but I didn't want it to happen to me! I thought we were gonna lose a lot more feel, and a lot of skill, if we couldn't do that. It really stuck in my head, that incident. After we got through the first verse, I said, 'Cut! Let's just go through our set.' I didn't say any more about it. But I could just tell that feel wasn't there."

The time for rebuilding her band would soon arrive, but, for the moment, the girl from Ohio was pleased to revel in the success of the occasion. Like many committed reactionaries in the music business, Chrissie had probably never realised the impact that a single rock concert *could* have. *Live Aid* had bowled her over and, in consequence, she became committed to the idea of 'using' performance in order to promote a series of ideological beliefs. Albeit she's been quick to realise – an awful lot quicker than most in fact – that the public's imagination wouldn't be caught so readily by a Live Aid Mark II.

"I don't know if anybody could really stomach any more *Live Aid* type of stuff," she observes. "But I'd still like to see people push this revolution along a little bit. I'm hell bent on stopping animal slaughter and that sort of stuff. It would be nice to think people could stop destroying and wrecking my world, and stop putting poison in the air and the water, and just generally wrecking the environment that I live in, and, y'know, pornography and all that stuff, and all that violence-related sort of crap.

"It would be really cool to see people start to walk into newsagents and just take all the smut off the racks and throw them in the street. God knows, I've threatened the guy across the road in my newsagent hundreds of times. Every time I walk in I say, 'This is a bust! When are you gonna get that smut off the shelves?' And I always wait until there's a shop full of people, and really embarrass them. But I'm not very brave, or I'd go in and set it on fire – but then everyone just thinks you're being a fanatic."

Back in Britain by the autumn then, Chrissie chickened-out, and left her matches at home every time she went for the Sunday paper. She would soon get the opportunity to do *something* positive for her fellow human beings however, when in November, the Nevada Del Ruiz volcano erupted, almost totally burying the Colombian town of Armero.

Having just made a guest appearance (the previous month) with UB40 at Glasgow's newly-built Scottish Exhibition Centre, Chrissie hadn't been planning much more live work until the re-emergence of her own band. But when the chance to put her pulling-power where her mouth was, there would clearly be no holding her.

In February 1986, Ms Hynde offered her services for the Colombian Appeal show, held at London's Royal Albert Hall. Also featuring the likes of Pete Townshend, Annie Lennox, Dave Gilmour, The Communards, Working Week and The Comic Strip team, the event was organised by Chucho Merchan, whom The Pretenders actually worked with on 'Get Close', the album they would release later that year.

Resisting the temptation to use such an occasion as a testing ground for new material, Chrissie – in company with Robbie McIntosh – delighted Pretenders fans in the audience with a rhythmic rendition of 'Back On The Chain Gang', and then followed it with the kind of song she'd never *normally* be able to perform – Bob Dylan's 'Property Of Jesus'.

A big fan of the Minnesota Minstrel since her teens – **"Actually Dylan and Ray Davies are out on their own in the big league of songwriting"** – it wouldn't surprise many people that she'd wanted to play one of the great man's songs, especially after she'd been welcomed on stage with him at Wembley Stadium the summer before *Live Aid*. What *did* come as a turn-up however, was that she chose *such* a song, a deeply religious number, snatched from the severely secular, and highly controversial album, 'Shot Of Love'. The fact is, of course, Chrissie has always been a closet Christian.

SINK OR SWIM: UB40 OFFER CHRISSIE CAREER ADVICE.

"**Oh yeah,**" she says somewhat matter of factly. "**I certainly believe in God. To me, at the risk of sounding like a new-born Christian, which I'm not – I've never doubted it and it's never left me for a moment. It's never been a question for me. To me it's the driving force throughout the day and night, that I'm, like, working for Him. This isn't anything new to me. I've also been a vegetarian for 15 years – these subjects aren't a matter of faddism, these are my personal beliefs, which are immovable. This is the foundation of the me that sits here today.**

"**I believe most of what's written in all those books about the prophets and all. I'm far more inclined to believe that the earth got into the form it's in now in seven days, rather than Darwin's theory. I don't think we evolved from monkeys. I don't buy that for one moment. It makes no sense whatsoever to me. Why did we come from monkeys? Why not ducks or dogs or sparrows? I think that humans are humans and monkeys are monkeys and never the twain shall meet . . .**"

With as many people confused about Chrissie's personal identity as there were critics uncertain about her band's future, it perhaps seems fitting that The Pretenders first single to appear in two years should be titled 'Don't Get Me Wrong'. We'd all be mistaken should we jump to any conclusions about that one though.

"**Ha-ha! I actually wrote that song for John McEnroe! He used to come to our gigs. He's a big rock 'n' roll fan and he plays the guitar – well, he's getting better – he plays a good solo, better than I can. I tried to coach him, but he's got a really stiff wrist, so I had to grab his arm and shake it real, *real* hard, saying, 'Come on, get your wrist loose, you'll never play with a wrist like that.' And the people with him were horrified. Because apparently his wrist has something to do with the way he plays tennis. So I don't know if I had anything to do with his sporting decline . . .**

"**Anyway, as I recall, he'd just pulled yet another obnoxious stunt on court. Being a feisty sort myself I always had a regard for John. Before I ever met him, I used his line 'You guys are the pits of the world' at the beginning of the second album. He was delighted. Later I heard he was trying to get a band together so I thought this song that went – 'Hey don't get me wrong, I'm misunderstood' – was ideal for him. He was too shy to sing it though. Then it got used in a film called *Gung Ho* which was about the communication problems between American and Japanese business people. It adapted fine, so everyone was pleased, even John.**"

With the help of an '*Avengers*-style' promotional video, which cast Chrissie as Emma Peel (significantly it was Farndon who had first made the comparison years before) alongside Patrick McNee's original John Steed, 'Don't Get Me Wrong' became the first Pretenders song in five years to reach the Top 10. And within a matter of weeks, by November 1986 in fact, the band's brand new album had imitated the single's success.

In a career of turning points, 'Get Close' proved the LP to break most ties with the past. Not because the material no longer sounded like The Pretenders, but simply because the band would cease to have any links with the outfit Chrissie Hynde had first put together for Dave Hill. Martin Chambers, the last surviving original Pretender at this stage, was soon to be dispatched to 'session musician' status.

"Martin was very sympathetic to my decision to try other people," remarked the leader. **"Although I don't think he was very happy about it, no, certainly not."**

A parent himself by now, Chambers probably thought it rather late in life for him to be changing horses mid-stream, and . . . yes, he was a bit miffed. Not least because he (quite understandably) felt he'd proved his worth long before the *Live Aid* rehearsal 'incident'. Needless to say he did accept the opportunity of appearing on the LP in a 'guesting' capacity though, as did Malcolm Foster who also appeared to be pensioned off.

Although the recording sessions featured a host of helpful extras, most notably Bernie Worrell, it was American drummer Blair Cunningham (of Haircut 100 and brief Echo And The Bunnymen fame) and bassist TM Stevens (jazz enthusiast and one-time James Brown extra) who cut through the crowd to establish themselves as The Pretenders' new rhythm section. Intended to provide the nucleus of a touring band for the next 12 months, however, the line-up would again be altered by the time they got on the road – with Malcolm Foster seemingly back in favour.

Of all the changes at this time, the one to attract the least attention, yet the one which perhaps was the most significant, was Chrissie Hynde's choice of producer. Gone was The Pretenders original fifth member, Chris Thomas, and in his place the coupling of Bob Clearmountain and Jimmy Iovine could be found sharing the credits. This, in spite of an earlier intention to employ Steve Lillywhite.

As for the songs, well, many critics considered it the strongest Pretenders collection to date, several singling out the poison-tipped 'How Much Did You Get For Your Soul?' as one of the songwriter's most scathing achievements.

"That was about the act of doing those endorsements for money and stuff," Chrissie explains, **"and in the song I just kinda used the black community in America – Whitney Houston, Michael Jackson,**

THE PRETENDERS 1987: L-R ROBBIE, BLAIR, CHRISSIE, KEYBOARD PLAYER RUPERT BLACK, AND MALCOLM – BACK IN DEMAND.

Lionel Richard or whatever his name is . . . And nothing's changed
. . . Aretha Franklin is doing Amoco gasoline adverts, Tina Turner's
doing a Pepsi ad – they're all doing these ads. And the point is, these
guys are all getting 15 million dollars to influence the young black
kids and encourage them to drink something that's not good for
them. And people might say, 'Well, Coke's not that bad – *you* drink
it', but the point is, it's one thing to do something and it's something
else to advertise it . . . Listen, I might smoke cigarettes, I might
inject heroin, but I'm not going to get up on television in front of
millions of people and tell them to do it too.

"Advertising is crap. And these guys are endorsing these stupid
products. Why would anyone who had any consciousness whatsoever
do an advertisement for Pepsi Cola? It's the crassest form of
pollution. People are going out and getting all that dough to endorse
some garbage product when they don't even need the money
anyway. What the fuck are you gonna do with 15 million dollars?
Buy a fleet of Rolls Royces? Pepsi Cola is a crap product. It has no
redeeming value whatsoever . . .

"And you know . . . any consumer product is obviously going to
be hurting somebody if it's only there for sense gratification. The
reason there's all these people starving – two thirds of the world – is
because of big companies like Pepsi Cola. It's not the only reason, but
it all adds up. So these guys who were in shackles for two hundred
years . . . you know, go back and pick cotton on the plantation pal,
because that's *exactly* what they're doing, they're *still* being
exploited by the white man to sell his goods. All these musicians are
doing adverts and jingles for Burger Chef and every other bullshit
product there is. It's sell, sell, sell. Well, you don't take 15 million
bucks to do a Pepsi advert around *me*, buddy boy!"

Chrissie Hynde has always liked to speak up for herself and her principles. Happily she's also prepared to speak up for her audience, a significant characteristic – as it turned out – the day her band were booked to play Brazil's *Rock In Rio* event, back in January 1987.

Scheduled to appear on the same bill as both Simple Minds *and* UB40, The Pretenders found themselves on-stage at the same time as a fight broke out between fans and a group of extraordinarily over-zealous security guards. Throwing her guitar to one side, the incensed rocker raced to the front of the stage and screamed **"No one fights at our shows!"** – and with that, the seemingly inevitable blood-bath was halted forthwith.

Back home there were few such problems as The Pretenders prepared to play their first batch of British dates with the new line-up. Opening a May tour at Glasgow's Barrowlands, their reviews were favourable enough to warrant the group's attachment to a handful of open-air dates with U2 later that summer. And although audiences still clamoured for them to play the old favourites, Chrissie was encouraged to hear requests for their most recent of releases, 'Hymn To Her' – a track for which she still harbours a special affection.

"That was written by an old friend from High School called Meg Keene," Chrissie tells us. **"I hadn't seen her in years, but a mutual friend played me some of her songs and they were great, real offbeat stuff.**

"At the time she was living on a commune in Missouri, making hammocks and nut butter. That all had a happy ending because, with all the money she made in royalties, she was suddenly able to adopt a blind Indian boy. I'm thrilled that performing a song can have that sort of repercussion."

By way of a follow-up to 'My Baby', one might have expected The Pretenders to release a fourth track from 'Get Close', as a summer single. Instead, they astounded the critics by recording, and releasing, a song from the soundtrack of 1987's new Bond movie, *The Living Daylights*. Entitled 'If There

"NO CAMERAS IN HERE BUSTER!" CHRISSIE SEARCHES SEAN PENN FOR OFFENSIVE WEAPONS.

Was A Man', the release attracted the obvious criticisms, which, somewhat surprisingly, Ms Hynde had failed to anticipate.

"Sexist?" she inquired at the time. **"007 sexist? Well, I must say, to be honest, I've never thought about it. I haven't seen all of the films, but I saw this one before I wrote the song, and I thought it was really good.**

"The thing with James Bond is that everyone *knows* he's this English secret agent who's got a flash car and likes women. He enjoys having a drink and getting a kick, which actually is a very traditional rock 'n' roll attitude – take that how you like – and I think that's what's attractive about him. You can excuse him some of the excesses because he was working hard and this could be his last night and all.

"But apart from that stuff . . . along with the gadgets and the chicks and everything, there's always been this great music that goes with it. 'Goldfinger' was a great song, y'know, in its time . . .

"Really, if there are things I *do* hate though, they aren't James Bond films – but tabloid newspapers. I absolutely detest everything they stand for and the way they put out their message every day and try to keep people stupid . . . If you're gonna get angry 'bout something, you'd do much better to get angry with them, y'know?"

Right now, Chrissie didn't have time to get angry with anything, mainly because her guitarist suddenly decided to leave, and she desperately needed a replacement in time for the autumn schedule – a US tour with U2.

"Robbie phoned me out of the blue," she recalls, **"and he just said, 'There's no point in beating around the bush, I've got to give it the elbow.' I was really shattered because I loved Robbie. He was a fantastic person to work with, always."**

Fantastic or otherwise, McIntosh wouldn't prove irreplaceable, and The Pretenders again fell on their feet when former Smiths' instrumentalist Johnny Marr showed a keen interest in signing up straight away. Soon after a handful of rehearsals with the rest of the line-up, it became abundantly clear the band couldn't possibly do any better.

"It's like being in love again," Chrissie exclaimed at the time. **"I haven't felt this good about the group since I met Jimmy Scott. Johnny grew up learning to play guitar by listening to a lot of Jimmy's stuff and they do have very similar sensibilities. It was instinctive asking him to join because, although I'd heard of The Smiths and loved 'Meat Is Murder', I wasn't honestly an expert about their music. I'm still not.**

"Johnny came over to my house and we went down to

The Marquee together, had a drink, went for a walk round Soho. It felt right. After carrying the band and being pushed towards a solo direction (a rare admission!) that I never wanted, I can concentrate again on the original Pretenders idiom . . . 'Us against the rest of the world.'

"That's a vital frame of mind for any group. The original incarnation *has* to agree on that. Later, sure, it degenerates – the singer hates the bass player, nobody talks to each other. That's why it was so groovy for The Smiths to quit while they were on top. They ended with integrity rather than allowing the rest of the world to witness a sordid relationship. No one likes it when an original member leaves, the public hates it and so do the musicians . . . People *know* what they like y'know."

Indeed they do, and one thing the people certainly seemed to like that year was the string of Stateside dates The Pretenders (complete with Johnny Marr) played with U2 during November.

Having sung backing vocals on U2's hit single 'Pride (In The Name Of Love)', Chrissie had always enjoyed the Irishmen's music, but had never fully appreciated their importance as a live act. Neither had she realised how entertaining the boys could be on a more personal level. Bono, especially, turned out to be a priceless companion on the road.

"He's just very funny," the Pretender explains. "He tells these jokes that aren't really funny, but when he tells them they're *very* funny for some reason. Let me think of one. Oh, I know – though of course I can't tell it as badly as he does – This sandwich walks into a pub, pushes his way through the punters and gets up to the bar and says, 'I'd like a Guinness', and the bartender says, 'I'm sorry, we don't serve sandwiches!'

"Bono's a good laugh . . . but he's probably not quite like most people might imagine him . . . I remember we went to a Richmond Cornejo show a while ago, and he was lusting after all the models, saying, 'See that one with the pale red hair, I could take her away from all this, I could save her.' His wife was there too. I looked at her, and she looked at me, and we both looked at him and just thought . . . Bono you're completely out of your tree . . .

"On the tour he used to come into my dressing room before the show and say, 'Hey, listen to this song I'm writing,' – some of them weren't very good, ha-ha! And when we first got to Rome – earlier on in the year – he came to my room and we stood out on the balcony, looking out over Rome, and he'd already got halfway through my mini-bar. He said his throat was bothering him, and did I have any

> BONO'S VERY FUNNY . . . I REMEMBER WE WENT TO A RICHMOND CORNEJO SHOW A WHILE AGO, AND HE WAS LUSTING AFTER ALL THE MODELS.

more brandy?! Every night he and the rest of U2 would be out till six o'clock in the morning, *always* clubbing."

Chrissie Hynde's fast-developing camaraderie with the Irish rockers wasn't simply a matter of on-the-road pleasantries however. With the seven-year itch turning up typically late in The Pretenders career, Chrissie had found herself with little left to dispose of that autumn. She *had* been with the same manager ever since the band's inception though, and so, without stopping to divulge all the sordid details to the press, Chrissie sacked Dave Hill, and replaced him with Paul McGuinness – manager of U2.

Whether or not there was a deliberate intention to draw a curtain over the band's career to date, The Pretenders brought out a nostalgic single in the form of 'Kid' (a remix, backed with the original demo version of 'Stop Your Sobbing'), specifically designed to promote 'The Singles Album' – which was made available just in time for the Christmas market. But if Santa welcomed the LP with open arms, Chrissie was less than chuffed with the release.

"Well, for one thing," she divulges, **"I never wanted 'I Got You Babe' on the album. It** *wasn't* **a Pretenders song, and its inclusion here was really a concession to the record company people who** *did* **want it included.**

"But also, I genuinely find it sad listening to some of that collection. Especially 'Message Of Love' and 'Back On The Chain Gang', the song that ends side one and closes that particular period. I find it sad listening to *those* **again, certainly. 'Message' was the first group's last shot, recorded in Paris. Jimmy Scott died before 'Chain Gang' of course, and Pete Farndon had left and was about to die . . . This whole time was a tremendous drag. It looked like curtains for the band. I never felt like packing it in, but my enthusiasm** *was* **waning, I have to admit it.**

"Maybe I give an impression of self-confidence, and people buy that. I've always bluffed my career really, but I'm able to persuade brilliant players to join me . . . so I guess that makes it all OK.

"When all's said and done, I'm proud of the fact that I managed to pull The Pretenders through. And I'm proud of the fact that I'm not going to swat a mosquito, even though it's in my power to do so. That's just the kind of guy I am.

"But there are regrets too, of course. Oh, a list as long as your arm of regrets. Obviously I regret the deaths of Pete and Jimmy. I do feel that I was partially guilty, that maybe I could have helped if I hadn't had my own personal problems at the time, and been so wrapped up in myself. And I regret a lot of my song lyrics, which I think were naff. In fact, most of my song lyrics I regret!"

CHAPTER SIX

Still Pretending

FACE LIFT: CHRISSIE RAISING HER PROFILE.

"If I had my time over again," ponders the last great Pretender, **"I think I'd give rock 'n' roll a miss. I'd learn to sing properly and I'd become an opera singer instead. Only thing is, I don't think I'd make a very convincing fat lady.**

"I'm actually very lucky to do what I do, and I know it. But there's a lot of associated bullshit. I don't mind being a voice, but I never wanted to be a face. I don't want to promote my product, I don't want to advertise my product. If you don't wear high heels and lipstick in this business pal, you'd better get on to a model agency quick. Huh! If it was up to me I'd get Yasmin Le Bon to go on the covers of all my albums, and I'd just call it a day.

"The thing is, we never were the most glamorous bunch of guys. Right from the start with the original band, none of us were like, the

greatest poseurs in the world. Photo sessions were usually a bit of a balls up, and we always looked like we were about to throw up or something. And videos, *videos*, they were even worse! We've done some pretty rotten videos – but I always thought that the charm of the band was that we looked pretty ugly. Particularly in this modern day and age where everybody's trying to look better and glossier all the time, it's nice to have a couple of 'ugs' in there to relate to."

Regardless of her own modest opinion, Chrissie's never been what you'd call the average 'ug'. Nor has she ever been the average pop star, come to that. Arriving in Britain the week that 'Tie A Yellow Ribbon Round The Old Oak Tree' topped the charts, she stayed – against the odds really – to develop and nurture a style of work that, if not significantly innovative, probably wouldn't, *couldn't*, have been provided by any other performer at such a time. And having given through her music, she'd then find time to give with her heart – to any deserving cause that would allow a foul-mouthed anglophile to represent it.

Over the last couple of years then, Chrissie has flirted with a variety of charitable and other, similarly worthwhile causes. In February 1988 she made a guest appearance at the Royal Albert Hall, for a show in aid of The Great Ormond Street Children's Hospital. A little while later she was seen to be active in the formation of an all-star vegetarian pressure group, 'Reprieve', aiming at **"an alternative voice to Britain's meat industry, which has millions of pounds to spend each year on advertising."** And at the end of last year her greatest challenge began when, as a director of the 'Ark' organisation, Chrissie became responsible for the development of an alternative fast-food chain, to rival the much-loathed McDonalds and its ilk.

Add to all this the great steps she's taken to help raise money for 'Lynx', the anti-fur organisation, as well as her involvement with the 'Rain Forest' appeal, and it soon becomes clear where her priorities lie.

"I've lost hours of sleep over the last 20 years – before which I was just a stupid girl – thinking about the Belsen for animals that exists all around us," Ms Hynde announces. **"Animal slaughter causes me a lot of sleep loss. The fact that we can take something else's life, and that some people think it's there to take, the fact that there's that kind of mentality so prominent in the world today . . . well, we don't really have a prayer.**

"People just don't care about the suffering of animals unless they see a dog run down by a truck, or a dog with its feet trussed up behind its back which happens to look like the dog they buy food for every day. Only then do people show compassion – but it's just cosmetic, it's a sentimental thing which I find really distasteful, despicable even. What else do I lose sleep over? The destruction of

DUAL IMAGE: THE PARTYING POP-STAR, AND THE SOCIAL ACTIVIST.

the planet. Waste. Plastic razors and lighters and all this crap which is thrown out in the garbage and burned. It's poisonous! That's one thing about doing those big festival type shows. I remember when we toured with U2 and everyone held up those goddam disposable lighters during their set – I kept wanting to run on-stage and give 'em all a quick lecture!"

Disposable lighters aside, Chrissie couldn't resist an invitation to take part in the birthday celebrations for Nelson Mandela (his 70th), when a celebratory rock gala was held at Wembley Stadium on June 11, 1988. Beamed by satellite all over the world, the show also featured Simple Minds, and was – as at least one national newspaper suggested – the closest Chrissie had ever been to making a political statement.

Although the question of fundamental human rights wouldn't be this author's idea of a party political issue, the notion does give rise to an interesting question however, and one which Chrissie has never been hesitant in responding to.

"The thing is, I don't *believe* in politics," she states with characteristic irreverence. **"And I don't think a political system can be affected by people. I think we can change the *system* though . . . Oh, I'm all for that, I'm completely anti-establishment. I'm part of the generation that, as the Vietnam War raged, rejected the values, the mundane world of our parents. I'm a hippie.**

"But y'know, so many of these problems are religious problems,

and not problems of the system at all. Capitalism is probably a good idea, but it can't essentially work because people are too greedy. They don't have an aesthetic sense, or a respect for the right things. They hoard. They'd rather destroy the environment outside to create an environment in the home. It's like Dallas, you actually go there and there's all that wealth, but there's nothing *beautiful*. America's not a very beautiful country.

"It all went wrong when they started killing the Indians. You can't lay a foundation on genocide and expect to ever thrive. It's the collective Karma that the country was founded on – murder. There's a lot to answer for there. And the whole slave system. There's too much that has to be reckoned with. Animal slaughter – it's murder! Abortion – it's murder! Essentially killing and basing your whole economy on it – which is the American way, whether they know it or not.

"Someone's got to draw the line and say you just can't do these things, someone who can not only foresee the consequences, but also sees that it's an unholy way to live. But nobody cares.

"It's a big problem, which gets worse the minute you realise that the whole of America has gotten out of control . . . The media – TV, newspapers – are incessant and hysterical. It seems like the whole country is brainwashed and people's consciousness has gone to sleep.

ARMS AND THE MAN: CHRISSIE AND ALI 'PERFORM' FOR THE GOSSIP WRITERS.

CHRISSIE: LEGGING IT.

Where are the black leaders? Where's Martin Luther King? Where's Malcolm X? Can you imagine Michael Jackson saying what LeRoi Jones said, 'Wake up niggers or you're dead!'? Somehow you can't say that after you've had a nose job!

"And the English are almost as bad, although in a slightly different way – *you're* just incredibly petty. Remember in this country when they first introduced the 20 pence coin, and it was on the front cover of all the newspapers, you remember, 'We Don't Want It!' Yeah, petty, that's the word. That's alright, but it's *not* alright when your petty-mindedness just allows you to sink into an ignorant muzz. If that's really where you're focused all the time, then they can be doing what the hell they like, left right and centre, screwing up the environment, and you're not even going to notice, let alone do anything about it. You're going to keep buying soap that's made out of animal fats, and never think about it, because you're too worried about what's going to happen on fuckin' *EastEnders* tonight!

"That's where most people are at, and that kinda pisses me off. If you ask most people if they'd rather be shot in the back of the head or the front of the face, they will choose the back of the head because they don't wanna see it coming.

"Just like most people wanna walk around in a haze and be appeased by the fact that they're gonna get a new car next month, or get laid this weekend, or whatever – just perpetrating their existence on these petty little gratifications and ignoring the *real* issues!"

The immediate issue for Chrissie Hynde in her role as a recording artist however, was to get another record out. And in view of the fact that her own group had entered another of their (almost mandatory) inoperative phases, who better to work with than UB40.

'Breakfast In Bed' was the result of this latest collaboration then, and although Pretenders fans might have found it bland by comparison to Chrissie's more traditional releases, enough people obviously enjoyed the song to make it a success.

With the record came the inevitable rumours of a developing relationship between Chrissie and the Brummie singer Ali Campbell, the major basis of which seemed to be firstly, that they knew each other, and secondly, that they were members of the opposite gender. In time however, the likelihood of there being any substance to the stories, escalated considerably as reports of estrangement in the Kerr camp grew almost daily.

By early 1989, the Simple Minds singer had reportedly confessed their marriage to be over, and certainly it seemed the couple had seen little of each other for some time – he preferring to remain in his beloved Scotland – she choosing to endure the seamier climes of the capital. The occasional weekend together never did seem a very steady basis for marriage, especially when the partners concerned appeared to have such a widely conflicting approach to their day-to-day existence.

"This is the thing I've discovered about Jim," Chrissie reveals. **"*I* think, 'I'm in a band and that's what I do, but that's not what I *am*.' But Jim thinks he's in a band, that's what he does and that's what he *is*. When he works with the band, he moves in with them. I might be an hour down the road, but he lives with them for two or three weeks. They make noise, he sits around, he writes, he's totally absorbed in it. When he records he *lives* with them. I come home every night and do my thing. I do my work, I get into it, then I come home. But you can't even *talk* to him the day of a show. He's totally there, that's his whole thing.**

"At first I couldn't work it out. Now I realise there isn't anything else in his life outside of that. Everything in his life has to be part of that Simple Minds experience. I'm not saying it's not right. But it *was* a dilemma for me for a while, because my approach to everything is to look so incredibly casual compared with him, that it could almost be interpreted that I've got no enthusiasm.

THE PRETENDER ON A RECENT VISIT TO MOSCOW.

"I don't care though. I used to say to him, 'I might be in a band, but that's not me.' But he was 18 when he got in a band. The band lifted his whole family from their meagre surroundings – clean out of the doldrums of their working-class set up. He's the Messiah of his family. Everything he does is channelled through his family. He does it all for his family. Whereas I _left_ my family to do my thing.

"Everything about us is like opposites. He doesn't want to exist out of that, and I _only_ want to exist out of that. Everyone he knows, he met because of the band – even me. Whereas nobody that I know has anything to do with The Pretenders. Meg Keene probably hasn't listened to _one_ Pretenders album!"

Truth will out, it probably wouldn't bother Chrissie if no one listened to a Pretenders album ever again. Certainly it wouldn't concern her should no one _buy_ another one. Indeed, of all the recording artistes who might make the claim, Ms Hynde is probably one of the few who really doesn't seem to live for the sake of her record company's bank account.

In an extraordinary television interview with Paul Gambaccini during the mid-1980s (_The Other Side Of The Tracks_), Chrissie actually recommended that Pretenders fans should save their hard-earned cash, and simply tape copies of their friends' records. Coming at a time when her industry was fighting bootleggers tooth and claw, the performer's remarks were considered tactless at best – scandalous and unacceptably provocative at worst. With the 1990s just around the corner, Chrissie is yet to change her tune.

"Home taping may be killing the music industry," she remarks, **" . . . but so let it. The producers that I've worked with, when I used to talk like that, they would just hang their heads and cry, because they all want their swimming pools and things. But I don't care . . . I really don't."**

For Chrissie Hynde, the whole pleasure of her position, is just being able to keep working, keep playing and keep being *involved* with music. **"I'm just one of those people who can't understand other people – the ones who make a living out of music but aren't enthusiastic. To me, pop music just makes life so much more fun,"** she claims.

"Just because I don't appear to be very prolific, it doesn't mean I'm not having a good time . . . I could step up my output, but who would want it? I just don't think people need new product from me any more than every three years."

As if to prove the point, The Pretenders first UK single of 1989 was, in fact, recorded the previous year. Plucked from the soundtrack of the *1969* movie, 'Windows Of The World' represented the first vinyl evidence of the liaison with Johnny Marr, having actually been cut during the time of the group's American trek with U2.

And as the world's press gathered for the unveiling of a new album, and line-up, that would take The Pretenders into another decade, Chrissie Hynde still found herself shrinking from the publicity machine surrounding her, still harking on the self-deprecating stance that has made her much *more* than just a woman of her time.

"I haven't gotten here on the wings of a dove, y'know," she says shaking her head. **"I wouldn't look to me, or admire me, if *I* was someone out there. The Chrissie Hynde Story is not a pretty picture.**

"But if people are looking for some kind of statement . . . Well, I think probably the greatest thing you can do in life, if you've got children, is to stay at home and look after them as much as you can. That's my ideal, and I wouldn't want to inspire anyone to let that end of things down . . .

"As far as the drug thing goes . . . obviously I wouldn't wish to endorse any kind of drug. The fact that half my band died of drug overdoses and a lot of other friends too . . . What do I have to say? But it's easy for me to get up and say, don't do any of these things. I know, because I've tried them all."

Chrissie Hynde is 38.

PRETENDERS DISCOGRAPHY

SINGLES

Stop Your Sobbing The Wait
Real ARE 6 January 1979

Kid Tattooed Love Boys
Real ARE 9 June 1979

Brass In Pocket Swinging London / Nervous But Shy
Real ARE 11 November 1979

Talk Of The Town Cuban Slide
Real ARE 12 March 1980

Message Of Love Porcelain
Real ARE 15 February 1981

Whatcha Gonna Do About It Stop Your Sobbing (demo)
Flexipop LYN 9650 April 1981 (free with *Flexipop* magazine)

Day After Day In The Sticks
Real ARE 17 August 1981

I Go To Sleep English Roses (live)
Real ARE 18 November 1981

I Go To Sleep English Roses (live) / Louie Louie (live)
Real ARE 18S November 1981 (A-side plays at 45rpm, B-side at 33rpm)

I Go To Sleep English Roses (live) / Louie Louie (live)
Real ARE 18T (12") November 1981

Back On The Chain Gang (parts 1 & 2)
Real ARE 19 September 1982

Back On The Chain Gang (parts 1 & 2) My Cities
Real ARE 19T (12") September 1982

2000 Miles Fast Or Slow
Real ARE 20 November 1983

2000 Miles Fast Or Slow / Money (live)
Real ARE 20T (12") November 1983

Middle Of The Road Watching The Clothes
Real ARE 21 February 1984

Middle Of The Road Watching The Clothes
Real ARE 21T (12") February 1984

Thin Line Between Love And Hate
Time The Avenger
Real ARE 22 May 1984

Thin Line Between Love And Hate
Time The Avenger / Bad Boys Get Spanked
Real ARE 22T (12") May 1984

Don't Get Me Wrong Dance
Sire YZ 85 September 1986

Don't Get Me Wrong Dance (extended version)
Sire YZ 85T (12") September 1986

Hymn To Her (remix) Room Full Of Mirrors
Sire YZ 93 December 1986

Hymn To Her (LP version) Room Full Of Mirrors (extended version)
Sire YZ 93T (12") December 1986

My Baby Tradition Of Love
Sire YZ 110 March 1987

My Baby Tradition Of Love (extended version)
Sire YZ 110T (12") March 1987

If There Was A Man Into Vienna
Sire YZ 149 August 1987
(credited to 'Pretenders For 007')

If There Was A Man Into Vienna
Sire YZ 149T (12") August 1987
(credited as above)

Kid (remix) Stop Your Sobbing (demo)
Sire YZ 156 November 1987

Kid (extended remix) Stop Your Sobbing (demo) / Whatcha Gonna Do About It
Sire YZ 156T (12") November 1987

CHRISSIE HYNDE / UB40 SINGLES

I Got You Babe
DEP Intl. DEP 20 July 1985
(Chrissie Hynde appears on A-side only)

Breakfast In Bed
DEP Intl. DEP 29 June 1988
(Chrissie Hynde appears on A-side only)

LPs AND CDs

THE PRETENDERS
Precious / The Phone Call / Up To The Neck / Tattooed Love Boys / Space Invader / The Wait / Stop Your Sobbin' / Kid / Private Life / Lovers Of Today / Brass In Pocket / Mystery Achievement
Real RAL 3 January 1980
(CD release on Sire K2-56774, 1983)

THE PRETENDERS II
The Adultress / Bad Boys Get Spanked / Message Of Love / I Go To Sleep / Birds Of Paradise / Talk Of The Town / Pack It Up / Waste Not Want Not / Day After Day / Jealous Dogs / The English Rose / Louie Louie
Real SRK 3572 August 1981
(CD release on Sire 256924-2, November 1986)

LEARNING TO CRAWL
Middle Of The Road / Back On the Chain Gang / Time The Avenger / Show Me / Watching The Clothes / Thumbelina / My City Was Gone / Thin Line Between Love And Hate / I Hurt You / 2000 Miles
Sire WX 2 January 1984
(CD release on Sire 923980-2, July 1984)

GET CLOSE
My Baby / When I Change My Life / Light Of The Moon / Dance / Tradition Of Love / Don't Get Me Wrong / I Remember You / How Much Did You Get For Your Soul / Chill Factor / Hymn To Her / Room Full Of Mirrors
Sire WX 64 October 1986
(CD release on Sire 240976-2 same date)

INTERVIEW PICTURE DISC
Baktabak BAK 2027 May 1987

THE SINGLES
Stop Your Sobbin' / Kid / Brass In Pocket / Talk Of The Town / I Go To Sleep / Day After Day / Message Of Love / Back On The Chain Gang / Middle Of The Road / 2000 Miles / Show Me / Thin Line Between Love And Hate / Don't Get Me Wrong / Hymn To Her / My Baby / I Got You Babe (with UB40)
Sire WX 134 October 1987
(CD release on Sire 242229-2 same date)

IMPORTS AND COMPILATIONS

THE PRETENDERS
US Sire MINI 3563 March 1981
(12" EP includes live version of 'Precious')

CONCERTS FOR KAMPUCHEA
Atlantic K 60153 April 1981
(Includes three tracks by The Pretenders)

THE LIVING DAYLIGHTS
WEA WX 111 August 1987
(Film soundtrack – includes two tracks by The Pretenders)

VIDEO

THE SINGLES
Track listing as 'The Singles' LP plus 'Whatcha Gonna Do About It'
WEA K 2422303 December 1987